A Necessary Engagement

PRINCETON STUDIES IN MUSLIM POLITICS

Series Editors: Dale F. Eickelman and Augustus Richard Norton

Diane Singerman, *Avenues of Participation: Family, Politics, and Networks in Urban Quarters of Cairo*

Tone Bringa, *Being Muslim the Bosnian Way: Identity and Community in a Central Bosnian Village*

Dale F. Eickelman and James Piscatori, *Muslim Politics*

Bruce B. Lawrence, *Shattering the Myth: Islam beyond Violence*

Ziba Mir-Hosseini, *Islam and Gender: The Religious Debate in Contemporary Iran*

Robert W. Hefner, *Civil Islam: Muslims and Democratization in Indonesia*

Muhammad Qasim Zaman, *The Ulama in Contemporary Islam: Custodians of Change*

Michael G. Peletz, *Islamic Modern: Religious Courts and Cultural Politics in Malaysia*

Oskar Verkaaik, *Migrants and Militants: Fun and Urban Violence in Pakistan*

Laetitia Bucaille, *Growing up Palestinian: Israeli Occupation and the Intifada Generation*

Robert W. Hefner, editor, *Remaking Muslim Politics: Pluralism, Contestation, Democratization*

Lara Deeb, *An Enchanted Modern: Gender and Public Piety in Shi'i Lebanon*

Roxanne L. Euben, *Journeys to the Other Shore: Muslim and Western Travelers in Search of Knowledge*

Robert W. Hefner and Muhammad Qasim Zaman, eds., *Schooling Islam: The Culture and Politics of Modern Muslim Education*

Loren D. Lybarger, *Identity and Religion in Palestine: The Struggle between Islamism and Secularism in the Occupied Territories*

Bruce K. Rutherford, *Egypt after Mubarak: Liberalism, Islam, and Democracy in the Arab World*

A Necessary Engagement

REINVENTING AMERICA'S RELATIONS
WITH THE MUSLIM WORLD

Emile A. Nakhleh

PRINCETON UNIVERSITY PRESS

PRINCETON AND OXFORD

Published by Princeton University Press, 41 William Street,
Princeton, New Jersey 08540

In the United Kingdom: Princeton University Press, 6 Oxford Street,
Woodstock, Oxfordshire OX20 1TW

Library of Congress Cataloging-in-Publication Data

Nakhleh, Emile A., 1938–
A necessary engagement : reinventing America's relations
with the Muslim world / Emile A. Nakhleh.
p. cm. — (Princeton studies in Muslim politics)
Includes index.
ISBN 978-0-691-13525-0 (hardcover : alk. paper)   1. United States—Relations—
Islamic countries.   2. Islamic countries—Relations—United States.   I. Title.
JZ1480.A55N35 2009
327.73017′67—dc22   2008040378

British Library Cataloging-in-Publication Data is available

This book has been composed in Minion Pro

Printed on acid-free paper. ∞

press.princeton.edu

Printed in the United States of America

3 5 7 9 10 8 6 4 2

To My Wife Ilonka

*Whose love, friendship, and support
made this book possible*

CONTENTS

AUTHOR'S NOTE

THIS BOOK'S ANALYSIS of political Islam and Islamic activism is informed by the author's experience at the Central Intelligence Agency, his expertise in Islam, the rise of Islamization in the past two decades, and discussions with Muslim interlocutors across the Muslim world. Thus, it is not a work of scholarship in the traditional sense, although it is intended to contribute to scholarship, policy, and a wider understanding of the role of political intelligence in policy decisions.

The book offers a blueprint, with specific recommendations, about how to design a public diplomacy directed toward Muslims; the ideas and arguments presented in the book are intended to contribute to a national debate on relations between the United States and Islamic countries. Hence, the book is written for policymakers, students of Islam, and an educated general audience, both in the United States and overseas. I do not follow the traditional scholarly method of quoting sources and footnoting although in a separate section I cite the sources consulted while writing the book, including newspaper reports, magazine articles, and public opinion polls. I acknowledge some people who helped me during the writing and production of the book but do not mention the names of three groups of people I had the privilege to interview and work with in recent years: Muslim interlocutors across the Islamic world; policymakers, diplomats, and field intelligence officers; and my former colleagues in the intelligence community and elsewhere.

The book uses such terms as "political Islam" and "Islamization" to describe the process of Muslims discovering their Islamic identity and acting in light of that discovery. The book does not use the terms "Islamist," "Islamists," "Islamism," or "fundamentalism," because in the author's view these terms are mostly media creations that do not constructively inform the debate about this phenomenon; instead, the author uses the more descriptive terms "Islamic activists" and "Islamic activism." The terms "Jihadists" and "radical Salafis" are used in the book to describe those who advocate, condone, and participate in violence and terrorism. "Wahhabism" describes a narrow, exclusivist, and particularly Sunni interpretation of Islam prevalent mostly in Saudi Arabia. The book also uses a number of Arabic words where appropriate in order to further explain the English usage or to inform the reader of the original word used by Muslim activists and interlocutors. "Islamic" and "Muslim" are used interchangeably throughout the book. I have also followed a simplified spelling of Arabic words such as *Sharia*. Shia is used in one form only; no "Shi'ites" or "Shias" are used in the book.

On a personal note, I was born in Galilee, north of Nazareth in Palestine, and was raised a Greek Catholic. I emigrated from Israel to the United States almost half a century ago. I went to a Franciscan high school in Nazareth, a Benedictine university in Minnesota for the B.A., a Jesuit university in Washington, D.C., for the M.A., and was awarded the Ph.D. from the American University in Washington, D.C. I taught at a Catholic college in Maryland for twenty-six years before entering government service as a Scholar in Residence at the Central Intelligence Agency. I retired from the U.S. government on June 30, 2006.

All statements of fact, opinion, or analysis expressed are those of the author and do not reflect the official positions or views of the CIA or any other U.S. government agency. Nothing in the contents should be construed as implying U.S. government authentication of information or CIA endorsement of the author's views. This material has been reviewed by the CIA to prevent the disclosure of classified information.

INTRODUCTION

MY EXPERIENCES at the Central Intelligence Agency and within the corridors of power in the nation's capital as director and senior analyst of political Islam and often solo briefer to senior policymakers on both ends of Pennsylvania Avenue confirmed my suspicions that our government lacks deep knowledge of the Islamic world and of the diverse ways Muslims understand their faith, their relations with each other, and their vision of, and attitudes toward, the non-Muslim world. According to media reports and public opinion polls, many Muslims believe that the U.S. government continues to view the Islamic world through the prism of terrorism, and many senior policymakers remain unwilling to entertain the notion that vast majorities of the world's 1.4 billion Muslims do not support terrorism or that many Muslims support ideas of good governance and are in fact ready and willing to enter into productive dialogue with the United States.

While standing at a book stall in downtown Amman and discussing with the bookseller the available titles on every conceivable Islamic topic, he turned to me and said, "If American leaders read half of these books; they would not be attacking Muslims all over the world. They would be speaking to us instead."

To deepen my expertise and strengthen my analysis of political Islam, I visited more than thirty Muslim countries in sub-Saharan Africa (Nigeria, Senegal, Ivory Coast, Uganda, Kenya, and Ethiopia), in the Middle East and North Africa (Egypt, Jordan, Lebanon, Syria, Israel, Palestine, Kuwait, Bahrain, the United Arab Emirates, Morocco, Algeria, Tunisia, and Libya), in South Asia (Afghanistan, India, and Pakistan), in Southeast Asia (Indonesia, Malaysia, Thailand, Singapore, and Australia), in Central Asia (Kazakhstan, Kyrgyzstan, Uzbekistan, and Turkmenistan), and in the Balkans (Albania, Macedonia, and Bosnia-Herzegovina). I also visited several European countries that have Muslim populations, which in recent years have witnessed a significant growth of Islamic activism. These visits allowed me the opportunity to engage hundreds of Muslims—thinkers, writers, activists, journalists, politicians, clerics, nongovernmental organization (NGO) workers, jihadists, liberals, radicals, Sunnis, Shia, and Sufis—in conversations on what is happening in the Islamic world. Most foreign government officials were aware of my employment identity; however, I often presented myself to typical Muslim interlocutors as an American scholar of Islam who consulted with the U.S. government on this issue. Many of them responded positively to my questions because I conducted the conversation in Arabic. When visiting a fifteenth-century mosque in Samarkand, speaking to an Islamic activist in Amman, cooling off inside the Umayyad mosque in Damascus, or conversing with a Hizb al-Tahrir radical leader in Jakarta, I received the clear and consistent message that Musims—especially the well-educated and professional middle classes—are increasingly troubled by present relations between the United States and the Islamic world and even more concerned about the future of these relations. Indeed, recent Pew, Gallup, State Department, BBC, University of Maryland, Zogby, and other public opinion polls bear out the fact that America's standing in Arab and Muslim countries in the past half decade has reached an all-time low.

I detected these trends soon after 9/11 and made vigorous efforts to highlight the need for a comprehensive, multipronged, creative, and long-range public diplomacy initiative in the Muslim world. Only token steps have been taken in this direction, and clearly much still needs to be done. A public diplomacy effort by the United States that is imaginative and clear could go a long way toward improving America's poor relations with Arabs and Muslims. President George W. Bush's announcement in June 2007 that he would appoint a special envoy to the Organization of the Islamic Conference (OIC) is a step in the right direction. On March 5, 2008, the president appointed Mr. Sada Cumber of Texas as a special envoy to the OIC and indicated that the new envoy will serve until the end of the administration's term. In fact, Arab and Muslim media reports in the past five years have indicated that appointing a distinguished American Muslim as ambassador to the OIC would resonate well with Muslims worldwide. This step should be one of many that America needs to take to restore its good relations with the Muslim world in the coming years. In chapter 4, I offer nine other recommendations that could serve as a public diplomacy blueprint for the United States.

Although the book analyzes U.S. policy toward the Islamic world in recent years, especially since 9/11, it does not engage in "policy bashing"; instead, it offers a forward-looking road map that focuses on engaging Arabs and Muslims rather than a backward-looking critique. Three assumptions underpin the book's proposed plan for effective public diplomacy: first, winning the hearts and minds of Arabs and Muslims is a generational challenge that requires a thorough knowledge of Arab and Muslim cultures and a long-term commitment in resources and personnel; second, the success of such an effort will be slow in coming, incremental, and hard to measure; and, third, the current low standing of the United States in most Arab and Muslim countries can be reversed. It may seem hard to believe today, but less than a generation ago the United States enjoyed warm relations with Arab and Muslim governments and publics—politically, economically, culturally, and educationally. Tens of thousands of Arab and Muslim students and professionals studied in and visited this country, and correspondingly thousands of American graduate students and scholars did research in dozens of Arab and Muslim countries, under the auspices of the Fulbright and similar educational exchange programs.

The book also argues that effective public diplomacy must be a unified effort pursued at the federal government level, driven by a presidential declaration that reaches out to Arab and Muslim publics. Such an initiative serves the national security of the United States and is essential to the country's ability to pursue its national interest. In order to isolate the terrorists and extremists as a fringe element among Muslims, the United States must reach out to the majority of Muslims with ideas of good governance—transparency, a genuine commitment to democracy, accountability, fairness, support of human rights and the rule of law, and opposition to repression—and policies that reflect balance, justice, and fairness.

Another part of the book's central thesis is that relations with the Arab Muslim world cannot be grounded mostly or exclusively in military and security policy. The United States in recent years, but especially since the terrorist attacks on September 11, 2001, has relied heavily on the use of force in Muslim lands to achieve its objectives—directly, as in Afghanistan and Iraq, or by proxy, as in Lebanon, Palestine, and Pakistan—and on threats to use force as a tool of regime change (with respect to Iran or Syria). Arabs and Muslims perceive this continued reliance on force and threat to use force as contrary to any serious and sustained engagement with the Muslim world.

Many Muslim interlocutors told me they consider the occupation of Iraq and the bellicose rhetoric toward Iran as a twenty-first-century version of the British and French colonial wars of the nineteenth and twentieth centuries and a modern version of the Crusades. Napoleon occupied Egypt in 1798, the British and the French divided up the Middle East between them in the Sykes-Picot agreement of 1916, British and French mandates were established over the region after World War I, Israel took over Palestine after World War II, and now the Americans are in Baghdad. A Muslim interlocutor told me, "You can't conduct public diplomacy through the barrel of a gun; boots on the ground might bring you military victory but won't win hearts and minds." Another one added, "We have heard a lot of speeches on reaching out to Muslims, but where is the beef?" Numerous public opinion polls have shown and recent Arab media reports have asserted that American public diplomacy cannot possibly succeed unless the U.S.-led occupation of Iraq is ended, the military operations in Afghanistan are scaled back, Guantanamo is closed, and the secret renditions and "torture" of Muslim prisoners are halted. A Muslim interlocutor said, "How can the Americans talk about peace, the rule of law, and human dignity when they constantly wage war against Muslim countries, incarcerate Muslims, and violate their human dignity and legal rights at whim?" According to Arab and Muslim media reports, the final step the U.S. government should take toward reestablishing American credibility in the Muslim world is to bring those officials who have abused Muslim prisoners or who have violated the law to justice. Unless these officials are held accountable, to many Arabs and Muslims, American advocacy of the rule of law in Muslim lands will ring hollow.

Because a successful public diplomacy cannot be made in a vacuum, the book offers a wide-ranging analysis of political Islam and the role of the intelligence community, especially the Central Intelligence Agency, in enhancing government expertise in political Islam and the growing Islamization of Muslim societies. Chapter 1 analyzes the nature, evolution, and challenges of political Islam; the causes that contributed to the growth of Islamization and the rise of radicalism; the political and theological diversity and conflicts within the Islamic world; the manifestations and drivers of Islamic activism; and the growth, ideologies, and performance of Islamic political parties, Shia political revival, and America's response to these developments. Political Islam, as used in this book, covers the actions of individuals and groups, lawful and unlawful, to change the political, legal, economic, educational, and judicial nature of public policy in their societies according to the activists' interpretations of their faith. The analysis in this chapter is informed primarily by the author's discussions and interviews with hundreds of Muslim interlocutors and activists on numerous visits he took to Muslim countries in the past decade and a half.

Chapter 2, on intelligence, details how the intelligence community has viewed political Islam, how it has collected and reported on it, and the tensions between the intelligence community and senior policymakers on political Islam and Islamic radicalism. Since the terrorist attacks in the United States on September 11, 2001, the intelligence community, especially the CIA, has worked diligently to deepen its expertise in Islam and inform policymakers of the realities of the Muslim world. The Central Intelligence Agency in the past two decades was the only U.S. government entity that actively pursued the development and nurturing of expertise in political Islam and the processes of Islamization and radicalization in Muslim societies. The CIA's Directorate of Intelligence, in particular, has spent time and resources to enhance this expertise among its analytic cadre, consciously and systematically. The commitment in resources and personnel was based on a simple but powerful assumption that American engagement with the Muslim world is a long-term proposition and that acquiring expertise in this area serves the national interest of the United States.

Such expertise, CIA leaders correctly concluded, must be interdisciplinary, covering executive decision making, economics, history, leadership dynamics and motivations, politics, societal forces, languages, cultures, civil society, and public opinion and attitudes. I analyze the different means the agency uses to build analytic expertise on political Islam, including academic outreach, language training, travels to Muslim countries, and information from open sources. Expertise also extends to the craft of analysis, including methodology, and the examination of assumptions, mind-sets, and scenarios.

The chapter also examines a series of policy issues, ranging from Iraq to democratization, the briefings the CIA offered to policymakers, and the ensuing tensions between intelligence and policy. Although the book highlights the CIA's role in this area, it is not an apologia of the agency or of the intelligence community. The book hopes to offer a balanced and nuanced account of political Islam as a generational challenge facing the United States and reflects the author's fifteen-year experience at the Central Intelligence Agency as a scholar in residence, a senior analyst and manager, and a briefer on political Islam.

As chapters 3 and 4 indicate, a successful public diplomacy initiative in the Muslim world must consist of a clear, simple, consistent, and well-articulated message and a set of core themes—a single narrative that highlights common interests between the United States and the Muslim world. The message should be tailor-made for specific Muslim audiences and spoken with one voice. The aim is to convince Muslims that fighting terrorism is not the same thing as waging war against Islam and that the United States and Muslim societies share many values in common, ranging from respect for human dignity to yearning for freedom, progress, and the betterment of one's life. Muslims and non-Muslims alike have suffered at the hands of terrorists and suicide bombers; in fact, more Muslims have been killed and maimed by acts of terror in the name of Islam than non-Muslims. Other key objectives of the message should be to spread ideas of good governance and the rule of law, undercut radical and extremist messages, empower forces of moderation and tolerance, and support democratization and political reform through peaceful means.

Moderate Arab and Muslim thinkers have maintained that effective public diplomacy should also involve credible local leaders and reformers committed to the rule of law and gradual change. These would include the leaders of mainstream Islamic political parties and movements—such as the Muslim Brotherhood (MB) in Egypt and elsewhere, elements of Hamas in Palestine and Hizballah in Lebanon, the Islamic Action Front in Jordan, the Islamic Constitutional Movement in Kuwait, the Wifaq in Bahrain, the Islamic Party of Malaysia, the Prosperous Justice Party in Indonesia, and Justice and Development Party (AKP) in Turkey—that advocate a centrist (*wasatiyya*) politico-religious ideology and are committed to nonviolence and gradual change.

The American government has refused to engage some of these groups despite their frequent affirmation of their commitment to the democratic process and to gradual change through the ballot box and their frequent participation in national elections. Other privileged interlocutors would include grass-roots Islamic NGOs and community workers, grade school and high school teachers, print and electronic media editorialists and writers, and young clerics, especially those working in small mosques and religious institutions in smaller towns and villages. The American Muslim community can be an effective interlocutor to the Muslim world and must be involved in public policy if we as a country are serious about reaching out to Muslims.

The United States should strive to cultivate a healthy relationship with the vast majority of these Muslims by pursuing a more sophisticated and nuanced approach based on expertise, understanding, dialogue, and a mutuality of interests. Its diplomatic initiative toward the Muslim world would neither preach to Muslims about what their religion "really" means or says nor exploit Sunni-Shia violence by favoring one sect over the other. Playing one sect against the other might serve our interests in the short run, but over the long haul such a tactic will foment sectarian violence and heighten Muslim suspicions that America is simply practicing the old colonial tactic of "divide and rule."

No matter how eloquent the message or how well choreographed the initiative, a new emphasis on public diplomacy toward the Muslim world will not succeed without other serious foreign policy initiatives. "You cannot sell hot air," one Muslim commented to me. A successful effort to engage Muslims must be embedded in a foreign policy that promotes multilateralism, a resolution of regional conflicts such as the Palestinian-Israeli issue and Kashmir, intellectual exchanges across religions and cultures, dialogue with adversaries, and an end to wars of choice and other military adventures. Future policies aimed at Muslim engagement must convince Arabs and Muslims that the United States is committed to ending inhumane practices such as those perpetrated at Abu Ghraib and other detention prisons and interrogation centers, shutting down Guantanamo and repatriating all detainees who are no longer subject to investigation and judicial proceedings, and working with the Israelis and the Palestinians to end the plight of the Palestinian people under occupation. The United States should revisit the rhetoric of terrorism, much like what the post-Blair British government of Gordon Brown has done, with an eye toward dropping such phrases as the "war on terror" and "Islamic terrorism" from our lexicon, recognizing that vast majorities of Muslims abhor violence and terrorism. Terrorists should be branded as criminals whose heinous crimes against innocent civilians make them enemies of all humanity, Muslims and non-Muslims. The so-called war on terror should be transformed into a global hunt for criminals who have used their warped interpretation of religion as a justification for their criminality and *hiraba* (war on society). In order to resonate more widely and acquire more credibility, the new public diplomacy also must distinguish between terrorists and anti-regime, pro-democracy dissidents and between increased piety and radicalism. Growing piety does not equate with religious extremism.

This book aspires to make a vigorous public case for serious American public diplomacy in the Muslim world—a case based on knowledge of the Muslim world and grounded in intelligence and policy experience. It aspires to demystify intelligence analysis and to add value to the public discussion of America's long-term relations with the Islamic world. The book advances the central premise that because engaging the Muslim world serves the national security of the United States, America should discard the terrorism prism through which we have viewed the Muslim world since 9/11 and focus on the common interests that bind America and mainstream Muslims. There are millions of Muslims who are critical of specific U.S. policies, as public opinion polls have repeatedly shown, but who support ideas of good governance and democratic values. This book offers a critical analysis of Muslim attitudes toward the United States, the reasons behind the high American unfavorability ratings in polling data, the policy concerns expressed in these polls, and the caveats and challenges a new public diplomacy would entail.

A Necessary Engagement

Chapter 1

POLITICAL ISLAM AND ISLAMIZATION

ON MY VISITS to Muslim countries, which in the business are known as TDYs or temporary duty visits, I entered numerous mosques (my colleagues used to joke that my TDYs involved "mosque hopping" or "mosque crashing") and spoke to dozens of imams and 'ulama (religious scholars). My Muslim interlocutors in these countries included ordinary people, mainstream thinkers, writers, journalists, and academics, political party activists, NGO officials, "establishment" (mostly adhering to the government line) and nonestablishment clerics, pro-democracy advocates, radical thinkers and jihadists, businessmen, restaurateurs, taxi drivers, farmers, and booksellers. During these visits, I also met government officials and interacted with allied intelligence services in dozens of countries. The analysis of what follows is informed primarily by these many discussions and interviews.

The goal of these visits was threefold: first, to track the growth of Islamization and Islamic activism across many countries, to study their manifestations, and to identify the factors that drive them; second, to compare and contrast the growth of Islamic activism in different Muslim countries and to develop a useful sense of the stages of Islamic activism; and third, to analyze how Islamic activists from different cultures, races, and sects understand the phenomenon of Islamization and use it as a basis for their political, economic, and social activism. My research focused on seeking answers to a range of questions: What theological arguments do Muslims advance to justify their activism as Muslims and as citizens of Muslim and non-Muslim countries? Why do some activists turn to Islam as an identity anchor, whereas others turn to nationalism? What factors determine the type of religious ideology—moderate and tolerant or radical and intolerant—they espouse as a foundation for their newfound activism? At the conclusion of each visit, I made recommendations to senior policymakers on the long-term implications of Islamic activism and assessed whether such a phenomenon poses a short- or long-term threat to the United States and to friendly countries and regimes. As an intelligence officer, the author upheld the intelligence community's golden rule that intelligence officers do not make policy; they only inform it.

In talking to activists from various Islamic political parties—whether the Islamic Party of Malaysia, AKP in Turkey, Justice and Development in Morocco, the Muslim Brotherhood in Egypt and Jordan, the Islamic Movement in Israel, or Hamas in Palestine—I was especially interested in learning whether their commitment to participatory government and democracy represented a tactical ploy to get them to power or a strategic shift toward accepting "man-made" democracy. Some argued they were genuinely committed to a pluralist form of government in which minorities—religious (Sunni or Shia), ethnic, and racial—would be afforded equal opportunities; others were not so categorical. The key question our policymakers asked about Islamic political parties was, Were they committed to a gradual, peaceful process of change and have they disavowed violence and terrorism as a means of pursuing their political goals?

In my interviews with a variety of Muslim activists, mainstreamers and radicals, I attempted to trace the process of radicalization and how young people in a particular country or community make the transition from moderation and tolerance to radicalism, the factors that drive this transformation, and how some of them ultimately translate their acquired radicalization and "jihadization" into acts of terror. That is to say, how does a young man move from being a nonpracticing Muslim to becoming a devout and observant Muslim and from there to a stage where he could justify the use of violence as part of his jihad in the service of his faith and global Islamic causes? When I asked a young Pakistani why he was going to Kashmir to do jihad against the Indians, he answered, "Why not? Kashmir is part of Islamic jihad." Then I asked, if the opportunity presented itself for him to go to Chechnya to fight against the Russians, would he go? "Of course," he replied. I turned to his father for an explanation. He said that his son's "jihad" would help him serve Islam and would give him an opportunity to leave that small village and make something of himself. If he is "martyred" in the process, he would be rewarded in eternal life. This might be a typical case of how a young man goes through the process of transformation from being a "normal" or "unremarkable" kid to becoming a jihadist. He drops out or, if lucky, graduates from high school, cannot find a job, starts frequenting the neighborhood mosque, gets indoctrinated by an activist imam or a cleric about the "enemies" of Islam and the duty to do jihad, meets a like-minded group, and is given useful contacts, papers, and some cash to travel to Kashmir or other places to do jihad.

This young man and others like him become ready recruits for terrorism. The jihadist-terrorist tendency is strengthened as the young man arrives at his destination and begins to interact with other jihadists, from Pakistan and elsewhere. Training, linkages with individuals and networks, and ideological indoctrination continue as the young jihadist becomes more engrossed in what he is made to believe is a rightful struggle in the defense of the faith. Many Muslim interlocutors correctly pointed out to me that jihad was not synonymous with terrorism. They argued that despite the fact that many non-Muslims equate jihad with terrorism, most Muslims view jihad as a religious effort—for example, fasting, prayer, and almsgiving—which aims at bringing Muslims closer to God. A Muslim journalist told me, "Jihad has nothing to do with terrorism."

Most of the Muslims I met, especially those who are members of political parties, movements, or groups or who work for NGOs, expressed strong interest in participating in a democratic political process and would like to see the American government exert more pressure on their governments to allow Islamic parties and movements to participate in elections openly, freely, and without harassment. I heard these calls for a stronger American push for democratization loudest in Egypt, Syria, Tunisia, Algeria, Saudi Arabia, Uzbekistan, and Kenya. Islamic parties have already participated in elections in the Middle East, North Africa, and Asia, but in many countries—for example Egypt, Algeria, Jordan, Morocco, and Tunisia—the governments and their security services tightly control the electoral process and prescribe only a narrow space within which Islamic political parties can operate. These regimes often speak in the language of democracy but resist genuine calls for political reforms. They paint all opposition—secular and Islamic—with the same broad brush and either exclude them from the political process or co-opt them into acquiescence. The terrorist acts of September 11, 2001 gave many of these regimes an excuse to silence all forms of opposition in the name of fighting terrorism, and they have used their antiterrorism rhetoric to garner Western support of their repressive policies.

ISLAMIZATION AND ISLAMIC ACTIVISM

Beginning in the early 1990s, when I started my visits to Muslim countries, I began to sense a growing awareness among Muslims, individuals and groups, of their faith as a moral compass of their daily lives, a guide for their social interactions and political activism, and a basis of their worldview. Their Muslim identity became dominant over other identities and began to drive many of their political and other activities. The growth of this phenomenon, which has come to be known as Islamization, varies from one country to the next and from one Muslim community to the next. Islamization initially was more visible in Muslim majority countries but in a few years spread to Muslim minority countries. Islamic activists in different countries have offered diverse definitions of Islamization, depending on their religious ideologies, historical experiences, sectarian affiliations, and legal schools of thought to which they belong.

For many activists I spoke with, Islam is total way of life that encompasses faith, the world community, and the state, or what they call the three Ds in Arabic—*din* (faith), *dunya* (world), and *dawla* (state)—and some activists also maintain that Islam is the solution, or *Islam hua al-hal* in Arabic, to their social, political, and economic ills. "Islam is the solution" has been a major slogan in the election campaigns of several Islamic political parties, especially the Muslim Brotherhood in Egypt, the Islamic Action Front in Jordan, and in some cases the Islamic Party of

Malaysia. Some Islamic activists, especially the radicals, also believe that the political, military, and economic weaknesses of Muslims in the modern era are due to Muslims having strayed from Islam and followed non-Islamic ideologies and values and that the renewal and reform of Muslim societies can be achieved only through an Islamic system of government and law.

On a visit to Turkey in the mid-1990s, I had an interesting discussion with a leading thinker of the Islamic political party Refah about the nature of Islamization and its relevance to Turkish political life, especially as "laicist" or "secular" Turkey was striving to acquire membership in the European Union. He said he viewed Islam as the moral compass of Turkey regardless of the pervasive control of the military, under the direction of the Turkish General Staff, and that secular Kemalism, which was introduced by Mustapha Kemal Ataturk in the 1920s, is an aberration, not the norm. He argued that Kemalism never took root beyond the thin sliver of university-educated elites in the urban centers of Ankara and Istanbul and that Turkey has always been an Ottoman Muslim state. Maintaining that Turkey has very little in common with Europe, he claimed that over the centuries the relationship between the two sides has been one of conquest and conflict and that Turkey should look south toward the Arab Muslim world, not to the Christian north. "Islamization is a good thing for Muslims," he said, because it helps them rediscover their Islamic traditions and heritage.

Islamic activists who have been involved in territorial conflicts, either against their governments or against a foreign occupation, have viewed the rise of Islamization among Muslims as a vehicle to mobilize their human and financial resources in the fight for their territory, either to gain autonomy from the central government or to liberate it from a foreign occupation. Islamic activists in Mindanao in the Philippines, in Xinjian Province in China, and in Aceh in Indonesia, for example, have struggled for territorial autonomy, whereas activists in Chechnya, Palestine, and Lebanon (before the Israeli withdrawal in 2000) have worked to liberate their territory from a perceived foreign occupation. These activists viewed Islamization as a source of their territorial-nationalist jihad, not as a path to global jihad advocated by al-Qaʿida, Usama Bin Ladin, or his deputy Ayman al-Zawahiri.

Between the "territorial" activists and the global jihadists, there are some groups that focus on creating a *Sharia*-based society in specific regions of the world transcending individual states. These movements, which include Jemaʿa Islamiya in Southeast Asia, Hizb al-Tahrir in Central Asia and the Middle East, and the Islamic Movement of Uzbekistan, view Islamization as a vehicle in their struggle to establish Islamic communities in those parts of the world. They tend to be closer ideologically and operationally to the global jihad paradigm than to the nationalist jihads of Hamas, the Chechens, and others. Hizb al-Tahrir, in particular, strives for the restoration of the Islamic Caliphate.

Islamic activists in Indonesia, Egypt, Saudi Arabia, Pakistan, Tunisia, Nigeria, and Jordan, for example, use Islamization to force their political leadership, which is ostensibly Muslim, to act more in accordance with Islamic law or *Sharia*. Muslim interlocutors in these countries have told me over the years that they strongly object to the "un-Islamic" behavior of their leaders; however, as these activists have come to realize that they could not dislodge their rulers from office, especially with the growing strength of the military and the security forces, they have turned their activism toward Islamizing their society from below. During a visit to Egypt, a Muslim Brotherhood member told me, "You Islamize society from below and the regimes will follow." The statement reminded me of the American baseball field story: "You build it, and they will come!" The governor of the Zamfara state in northern Nigeria gave a similar rationalization for his decision to institute *Sharia* in his state in the late 1990s.

In addition to mainstream Islamic activists, radical segments of Muslim societies have also pushed Islamization among their followers. As indicated in numerous interviews, "radical" is used in this context to reflect an exclusivist, narrow-minded, and rigid view of Islam and support for aggressive jihad, including the use of force. Several of the interlocutors who considered themselves radical claimed they did not engage in violence or illegal forms of jihad, but neither did they condemn the use of violence to further their cause. Other radical interlocutors justified the use of violence against perceived enemies of Islam. To these radicals, Islamization is a means to defend the faith in the face of the onslaught by the infidels. Radicals, whether in Indonesia or Uzbekistan, agreed on a few key points: many Muslim rulers and regimes engage in an un-Islamic behavior; Muslims are obliged to fight and overthrow such regimes and their Muslim supporters; jihad against unbelievers—Muslims and non-Muslims—is a religious duty that must be pursued by all means, including violence; opposition to perceived illegitimate Muslim governments often extends to the official clergy and state-supported mosques; and, while this jihad is country-specific, it is part and parcel of a global jihad against all enemies of Islam, near and far.

A critical difference between mainstream activists and radical jihadists is their approach to change. Mainstreamers often said that they believe in gradual change through peaceful means, including the ballot box, and that if they concentrate their efforts on social change, for example in the areas of education and judiciary, society will ultimately become more *Sharia* friendly. By contrast, radical activists—whether at Guantanamo or in a comfortable hotel lounge in Jakarta—make it clear they have given up on gradual change because entrenched regimes will not allow meaningful change to occur and that the electoral process in many Arab and Muslim countries is a farcical game designed to placate the populace while maintaining the regime's hold on power. To the radicals, the collusion between many Muslim regimes and the enemies of Islam—presumably the United States and Israel—have made them apostates who should be removed from power.

When I asked a radical jihadist at Guantanamo what he planned to do if and when he is released, he answered without hesitation that he would continue his jihad against the United States and pro-U.S. regimes, ticking off the names of Mubarak of Egypt, Saleh of Yemen, Musharraf of Pakistan, the two Abdallahs of Saudi Arabia and Jordan, and Ben Ali of Tunisia. Other detainees at Guantanamo who were caught in the dragnet net after 9/11 did not share that jihadist's radical views against the United States or other countries. In a conversation I had with a Hizb al-Tahrir activist in Indonesia, he calmly told me over lunch that he justified the use of violence against the Americans and other enemies of Islam, even though such violence might lead to the killing of innocent bystanders. In his view, the United States and other Western countries have already employed this type of violence against Muslims throughout the Islamic world, including in Palestine, Afghanistan, Chechnya, and Iraq.

Those interviewed suggest that there is a growing rapprochement between secular and Islamic activists because of their similar opposition to regime-repressive policies and authoritarian rule and that Muslim Brotherhood ideology is pervasive among most Sunni political movements across the Muslim world, especially at the popular level where "establishment" 'ulama and clerics have very little influence. As a consequence of Saudi supported proselytization, however, a conservative Wahhabi form of Islamic ideology has also spread throughout the Muslim world in the past five decades, challenging mainstream Islamic ideology. Polling data indicate that majorities of Islamic activists are committed to gradual and peaceful change and do not necessarily view the Christian West as an implacable enemy. The radicals, on the other hand, who constitute only a small minority of Islamic activists, see no common ground either with non-Muslims or with tolerant and moderate Muslims. Islamic activist organizations are technologically savvy and have used the Internet, text messaging, and other high-tech devices to promote their agendas. The interviews further show that Muslim parliamentarians have become so comfortable with the whole process of legislative politics that they are adept at political compromise when needed to pass specific pieces of legislation.

STAGES OF ISLAMIZATION

By interviewing Islamic activists over the past decade and a half, I have detected a process of Islamization occurring in different

Muslim communities that can be divided into six stages. While seemingly linear, these stages do not assume that increased awareness of one's Islamic roots and piety will necessarily lead that individual to become a terrorist, but it does indicate that an Islamized environment might be conducive to further radicalization and terrorism.

First, an individual becomes more aware of his Islamic identity as a path to increased piety and a guide for action. Second, the individual begins to spread his Islamic commitment to the family and the immediate group to which he belongs. Third, Islamization expands to the larger society. In these three stages, where most Muslims find themselves, Islam is perceived as a moral compass in the daily lives of the individual, the family, and the community. An Islamized family usually becomes more observant of the tenets of Islam (the profession of faith, fasting, prayers, almsgiving, and *hajj*) and begins to dress more conservatively and traditionally and pay more attention to Islamic education for the children. These three stages for the most part focus on promoting an Islamically based value system but do not carry over into the political realm.

The fourth stage ushers in the political process of Islamic activism where activists embark on an effort to transform their political community into a more *Sharia*-friendly one. In tracking these efforts with my Muslim interlocutors, I concluded that Islamic activists begin to target the ministries of education and justice in order to ensure that educational curricula and textbooks are imbued with Islamic education, references to the Qur'an and the Hadith, Islamic history and traditions (especially the golden age of Islam), and Islam's contributions to knowledge. In the ministries of justice, Islamic activists strive to make *Sharia* the source of legislation and the basis for social interaction within the community and between Muslim states and the outside world. An examination of grade school and secondary school textbooks in several Muslim states reveals the tremendous influence of Islamic activist bureaucrats in shaping the curriculum. Saudi Arabia offers an extreme example of the pervasiveness of Islam throughout the curriculum—from religion to physics textbooks. In the Moroccan curriculum, on the other hand, Islamic references are found only in religion and Islamic history textbooks.

During this stage, Islamic activists' efforts to change the political system are for the most part peaceful and lawful. As one interlocutor said, "We want to work within the system regardless of the nature of the regime." A Turkish activist told me in Ankara that in the 1980s and 1990s, for example, the Turkish Islamic Refah Party advised college and university students who were receiving financial and housing assistance from the party to major in public administration, law enforcement, and sociology. Upon graduation, these students would be employed in the ministries of police, education, and justice as well as in welfare associations and nongovernmental organizations. The Turkish interlocutor praised this approach as a thoughtful long-term strategy to Islamize society from below. This approach was similarly pursued in several Arab and Islamic countries. In some cases where this occurred, the government might appoint a "modernizing" minister of education—the appointment of the minister of higher education in Kuwait in the early 1990s is one example—only to discover that his efforts were thwarted by conservative bureaucrats throughout the ministry. These bureaucrats would join forces with powerful and equally conservative clerics and religious leaders, creating a formidable coalition that the minister was helpless to overcome. I asked an interlocutor in Jordan to explain why Islamic activists had been so successful in penetrating these critical ministries. His response, which I thought was very telling, was that for years most regimes focused on the "power" ministries—defense, foreign affairs, and treasury—and ignored the "soft" ministries of education, judiciary, and social welfare. In a conversation with a cabinet member in a Gulf Arab country, he lamented that fact and said, "By the time we discovered what was happening, it was too late!"

The fifth stage of Islamization takes the previous stage a step further, leading to a confrontation with regimes, ideologically and politically. Initially, the challenge to regimes from growing Islamization is through the electoral process, as Islamic political parties and groups begin to demand the right to vote in fair and free elections and to organize into legally recognized entities. As many of these activists are harassed by regime security services and often jailed without charges, Islamic organizations begin to criticize the regime for repression and violation of human rights. When regimes in several Arab and Muslim states fail to respond to the peaceful demands of these groups, street demonstrations usually erupt, leading to confrontations with the police, more arrests, and more violations of human rights. Pakistan, Egypt, Kazakhstan, and Uzbekistan are illustrative examples of this type of confrontation. What usually begins as a lawful challenge to the regime invariably leads to violence. Regimes tend to view such challenges as undermining their legitimacy and a threat to their survival. Some regimes, as in Saudi Arabia, have attempted to undercut the Islamic challenge by brandishing their own Islamic credentials and their own commitment to the faith and by accusing the opposition of fomenting *fitna* or sedition. Some regimes went so far as to elicit a *fatwa* from a pro-regime cleric criticizing any and all opposition to the regime. An Islamic activist in Uzbekistan told me at a meeting several years ago, "we can't fight the regime; we can't fight regime clerics, but in the long run all of these actions by the regime reflect the regime's diminishing legitimacy and the justness of our cause." The brutal repression of Islamic activists in the Fergana Valley by the regime of Islam Karimov in 2006, which resulted in hundreds of people being killed, underscores the interlocutor's point.

Despite these confrontations during this stage, most Islamic activists remain committed to the belief that they could change the system from within. Pragmatically, they might not have other options to deal with regimes that are so authoritarian, so powerful, and so entrenched. However, a tiny minority of these activists gives up on the gradual-change strategy, loses hope in its ability to force the regime to endorse meaningful political reform, and opts for confrontation and violence. As one interlocutor in Egypt said, "It has become especially difficult since 9/11 to force the regime to democratize because the Mubarak regime has used terrorism as an excuse to thwart all political reform. In fact, human rights conditions have become much worse in Egypt and in several other Arab countries in recent years." The constitutional change that the government of Hosni Mubarak rammed through the Egyptian parliament in the spring of 2006 on the surface looked like a step on the road to political reform but in fact resulted in expanding the power of the executive.

The sixth stage of Islamization applies to those activists who no longer believe in the efficacy of gradual change and who have come to view violence as a legitimate tool of political, ideological, and religious action. In this stage, acts of violence are committed against specific Muslim regimes for their perceived un-Islamic behavior, against foreign occupation, and against the so-called global enemies of Islam. Although many of these violent extremists start their activity on the home front, they quickly find a common ground with the global radical ideology and begin to affiliate, at least ideologically, with al-Qaʻida. We witness in this stage a transition in the thinking of violent radicals; they no longer view conflicts in Palestine, Kashmir, Chechnya, and Iraq as discrete cases but as part and parcel of a perceived U.S.-led global war against Islam, which in return requires a global jihadist response. This argument, in fact, is the core of al-Qaʻida's ideology, globalized more readily through the Internet and other forms of electronic connectivity and linkages.

ISLAMIC ACTIVISM AND RADICALIZATION

The identification of extremists and terrorists with global Islamic causes began to form in the late 1990s and became much more energized after 9/11. To illustrate, during my travels to Muslim countries such as Nigeria, Indonesia, and Malaysia in the early to mid-1990s, I rarely heard any mention of the Palestinian conflict. However, by the late 1990s and the early part of the new century, Muslim interlocutors all over the Muslim world began to voice their support of the Palestinian, Afghan, Chechen, and Iraqi peoples and criticize U.S. policies toward those countries as un-Islamic. For radical Muslims, jihad became a sixth pillar of Islam, which has overshadowed other religious duties required by their faith. Although Usama Bin Ladin emerged in the 1990s as the most prominent articulator of the radical paradigm, the radical message was voiced by other al-Qaʿida spokesmen, including Bin Ladin's deputy Ayman al-Zawahiri (Egyptian) and Sulayman Abu al-Ghayth (Kuwaiti). Saudi and other Arab radical clerics and thinkers in the past twenty years who supported some aspects of the radical message included the following: Abdallah Azzam (Palestinian, co-founder of al-Qaʿida), Nasir bin Sulayman al-Umar (Saudi), Hamid al-Ali (Kuwaiti), Nasir bin Hamid al-Fahd (Saudi), Salman al-Awda (Saudi), Ali al-Khudayr (Saudi), Abu Muhammad al-Maqdisi (Palestinian), Hammud bin Uqla al-Shuʿaybi (Saudi), Sulayman bin Nasir al-Ulaywan (Saudi), Abd al-Rahman bin Nasir al-Barrak (Saudi), Safar al-Hawali (Saudi), Abd al-Aziz al-Jarbuʿ (Saudi), Umar Abd al-Rahman (Egyptian), and Harith Sulayman al-Dhari (Iraqi). Other thinkers, such as Yusif al-Qaradawi, endorsed parts of the radical jihadist message but not others. Many of these thinkers have relied on the writings of Ibn Taymiyya (a thirteenth- to fourteenth-century scholar who lived in Damascus), Muhammad ibn Abd al-Wahhab (an eighteenth-century Saudi scholar), Abu al-Alaʾ Mawdudi (a twentieth-century Muslim thinker and founder of Jamaʿat-i-Islam in South Asia), and Sayyid Qutb, a radical thinker of the Muslim Brotherhood who was executed by the Egyptian government in 1966.

Beginning with Bin Ladin's first *fatwa* declaring jihad against the United States in 1996, the radical message has focused on three key principles: first, Islam, as a faith and a territory, is under attack; second, the enemy consists of the Christian Crusaders headed by the United States, Zionism headed by Israel, and pro-U.S. Arab and Muslim regimes; and, third, jihad in all of its forms, means, and targets—including violence against innocent civilians—becomes a justified duty of all Muslims. In addition to the core message, some radicals view the war between Islam and the "infidels" as a millenarian battle between good and evil that will last until the "final days." Although radical ideas have had a long history in Islam, al-Qaʿida and its supporters have expanded the permissibility of targeting innocent civilians and the use of weapons of mass destruction.

Al-Qaʿida argues that it is permissible to kill civilians, in reciprocity and proportionality, if the enemy has killed Muslim civilians (Bin Ladin has frequently cited the killing of Palestinian, Afghan, and Iraqi women and children by "invading" forces as a justification of al-Qaʿidaʾs position). According to radical thinkers, if any one of the following conditions prevails, then Muslims would be justified in killing civilians: the enemy kills Muslim civilians on purpose; civilians have assisted the enemy in carrying out the war against Islam (this extends to a democracy where the electorate would be held culpable by voting for leaders who engage in wars against Muslims); the enemy hides behind civilians while waging war; and heavy weapons are used in the conflict that inflict casualties beyond specific military or other justifiable targets. Despite such expansive definitions, radical apologists often cite their commitment to the principle of proportionality in targeting civilians. They also justify committing violence against fellow Muslims because they have either left the faith and therefore became apostates or rejected the doctrine of *tawhid* (oneness of God) and became polytheists. Abd al-Wahhab cited several other "voiders" that could result in an automatic expulsion of a Muslim from Islam, including praying to, and seeking intercession of, other entities than God (which applies to the Sufis and some Shia who pray to saints); considering non-Islamic and other human laws as more superior to Islam; making fun of Islam or the Prophet Muhammad (such as the Danish cartoon controversy); and assisting infidels in attacks against Muslims.

ISLAMIC RADICALS AND WMD

Muslim thinkers in recent decades have justified the right of a Muslim state to acquire weapons of mass destruction (WMD), especially nuclear weapons, on the grounds of self-defense, against an enemy who already possesses nuclear weapons. Iran, for example, has cited Israel's possession of nuclear weapons, and Pakistan has cited India. In recent years, al-Qaʿida radical thinkers, however, have argued that nonstate groups, such as al-Qaʿida, are similarly entitled to acquire WMD in defense of Islam. In response to a question about al-Qaʿidaʾs potential use of WMD against the United States, Saudi radical Shaykh Nasir Bin Hamid al-Fahd issued in May 2003 a twenty-six-page religious opinion in Arabic titled *A Treatise on the Legal Status of Using Weapons of Mass Destruction.* Al-Fahd said he based his findings on pronouncements from senior jurists representing several strands of Islamic religious law, including the four major recognized schools in Sunni Islam (Maliki, Hanafi, Shafi'i, and Hanbali). The author found the use of such weapons permissible and specifically empowered people of authority engaged in jihad to determine if and when WMD should be used. He offered four central points in defense of his position.

First, "defining WMD as only nuclear, biological, and chemical weapons is unacceptable and a self-serving Western ruse, because massive use of conventional weapons and bombs has killed millions of men, women, and children. Distinctions based on international law, the Geneva Conventions, and the Human Rights Charter have no standing in Islamic law, which recognizes the Qur'an alone as the source of legislation." Second, "the West's possession and past use of WMD established a precedent, as evidenced by the U.S. nuclear bombing of Japan, the British use of chemical weapons against the Iraqis in World War I, and the development of such weapons in Israel's arsenal." Third, "indiscriminate killing of civilians by jihadists' weapons of mass destruction is permissible if civilians cannot be practically distinguished from others in warfare. If they are killed collaterally, there is nothing wrong with it. Jihad is not to be halted because of the presence of infidel women and children, and Muslims in target areas may be killed as well, if there is compelling necessity." Fourth, "prohibitions against massive destruction of property, or "sowing corruption in the land," according to the Qur'an, are not applicable when fighting the enemies of Islam. Whenever two causes of "corruption" conflict, it is agreed that one averts the greater by committing the lesser, meaning that the corruption caused by infidels' remaining in their state of unbelief and not entering the rule of Islam is greater than the "corruption" caused by devastating and destroying their territory. Al-Fahd was arrested after he issued the treatise, and while in Saudi jail, Saudi authorities claimed that he recanted the treatise; however, it is instructive to note that no Muslim state or nonstate group has denounced the treatise or spoken against its findings. Radical jihadists continue to quote it as a justification to acquire and use WMD in their fight on behalf of Islam. Apart from the theorizing of radical clerics and religious scholars, Bin Ladin's radical message continues to resonate among some Muslim youth primarily because of its simplicity, clarity, and repetitiveness. It is communicated to Muslims who have limited education, is devoid of complicated nuance, and is global in nature. It is also tied to opposition to specific U.S. policies in parts of the Muslim world with which alienated, angry, and unemployed Muslim youth could easily identify. Whenever Bin Ladin has issued an audio or video statement, he usually peppers it with short, selective quotations from the Qur'an, something that a young man can easily memorize. Of course, Qur'anic citations, although highly selective, give the message an aura of religious legitimacy in the eyes of potential recruits. Secular, college-educated, professional mainstream Muslims are often hesitant to challenge the radical message because of their generally limited knowledge of the Qur'an, their disagreement with the same U.S. policies that Bin Ladin cites (Palestine, Iraq, Kashmir, Afghanistan, etc.), their opposition to the same pro-U.S. authoritarian Arab and Muslim regimes frequently cited in Bin Ladin's messages, and their fear of retaliation by radicals. These moderate activists who reject the radical message have themselves been subjected to harassment and imprisonment by so-called moderate regimes and therefore have become reticent to speak out publicly against the Bin Ladin message lest they be accused of being either pro-regime or pro–United States. The end result is that in several Muslim countries only two overt paradigms seem to exist in society: the authoritarian model reflecting a dominant regime and the radical model representing those who claim to speak on behalf of Islam.

Moderate Muslim thinkers who have been speaking out against the radical paradigm have argued that relations between Muslims and non-Muslims should not necessarily be conflictive, as Bin Ladin has postulated; that the Qur'an, revealed to

Muhammad in seventh-century Arabia, must be transformed to fit Muslim life in a twenty-first-century globalized world; and that the classical boundaries separating the *dar al-Islam* (abode of Islam) from the *dar al-harb* (abode of war) have all but disappeared. Today, millions of Muslims live in non-Muslim countries, especially in the Christian West, and should be able to reconcile their faith and their citizenship in these countries. These thinkers—including Abdol Karim Soroush (Iran), Mohsen Kadivar (Iran), Muhammad Shahrur (Syria), Tariq Ramadan (Switzerland), Khalid Abu el-Fadl (United States), Abdullahi Ahmad al-Na'im (United States and Sudan), Muhammad Arkun (France and Algeria), Hasan Hanafi (Egypt), and others—have been critical of the radical message and have engaged in a new kind of reasoning *(ijtihad)* calling on fellow Muslims to embrace an inclusive and tolerant vision of Islam. They have also argued that certain aspects of Western political culture, including parliamentary democracy, political and social pluralism, women's rights, civil society, and human rights, are compatible with Islamic scriptures and traditions, maintaining that these aspects of modern democracy are in line with the position of the three great Muslim reformist thinkers of the late nineteenth and early twentieth centuries: Jamal al-Din al-Afghani, Rashid Rida, and Muhammad Abdu. Despite their modernist message, however, these thinkers seem to exert only limited influence among their co-religionists in the Muslim heartland. Many of them reside in Europe and the United States, write in foreign languages (English, French, German, or Dutch), and lack an effective organization to spread their message in the Arab world.

MANIFESTATIONS OF ISLAMIZATION

In the past fifteen years Islamization has been manifested in increased piety (mosque attendance, fasting, etc.), a return to traditional and more conservative garb, a significant expansion in the number of Qur'anic *madrasas* and Islamic schools, growing demands for the establishment of *Sharia* as the basis of governance, spread of Islamic publications, audio and video recordings of Friday sermons and other religious speeches, growth in satellite religious broadcasting, widespread Islamic political activism, energized proselytization, expansion in the number of international Islamic NGOs, and growing international linkages among Muslim activist individuals and groups. A Muslim academic interlocutor in Turkey told me several years back that he had never seen his co-religionists pray so frequently and so openly. "They even started to fast!"

The daughter of a Kuwaiti friend, who at the time was a college student, chided her college mates for "shedding blue jeans and donning the *aba* [a black outer garment]." She said she and her "liberal" and "more secular" friends understood the reasons why more Muslims were returning to traditional garb, but she did not think that totally covered women (whom she described as BMOs or "black moving objects") were necessarily better Muslims than those wearing Western clothes. Yet, traditional Islamic fashions have become a huge business, and major stores in Kuala Lumpur, Beirut, Ankara, Istanbul, Amman, Cairo, Rabat, and Jakarta have large displays of expensive floor-length dresses and *abas* for women. Silk and wool scarves and head covers (*hijabs*) of all colors and materials are also on display in high-end stores. To illustrate this transformation, only a few years ago a town in the Qasim region in the heart of Saudi Arabia was the only place in the Muslim world where one found totally covered women. In recent years, however, one could see such women in wealthy neighborhoods of Beirut, Cairo, Kuala Lumpur, and Rabat—and even in central London and by Lake Geneva.

Perhaps the four most noticeable manifestations of Islamization have been the spread of Islamic NGOs, the growth of Islamic schools, the global linkages among Islamic activist individuals and groups, and the Arabization of the Islamization process. Qur'anic schools, whether in a village in northern Nigeria or in the Fergana Valley in Uzbekistan, teach the Qur'an in Arabic. I watched little children in poor Nigerian hamlets recite *suras* (chapters) from the Qur'an by heart in Arabic and observed high school and college students at the Deoband University (Dar al-Ulum) outside New Delhi in India discuss different interpretations of the Hadith in Arabic. As a personal example of this phenomenon, I was able to converse with almost all of my Muslim interlocutors in Arabic regardless of where I was in non-Arabic-speaking Muslim countries, whether in Nigeria, Uganda, Kenya, Indonesia, Malaysia, India, Pakistan, Afghanistan, Pakistan, Central Asia, Turkey, or the Balkans. On a recent visit to the Balkans, I recall only one of the twenty-eight Muslim interlocutors I interviewed who could not converse in Arabic. The Arabization of Islamic proselytization, or *da'wa*, has developed despite the negative attitudes many non-Arab Muslims harbor for Muslim Arabs or Arab Islam. For example, I have heard Muslims in Indonesia and in Central Asia say that their brand of Islam is gentler than Arab Islam, and they resented the perceived condescending attitude of Muslim Arabs toward non-Arabs. The role of Saudi-supported proselytization in the Arabization of Islamization, especially since the early 1970s, should not be underestimated. An Uzbek interlocutor was speaking in Arabic while he was criticizing Arab Islam, and when I asked him where he studied Arabic, he replied, "at the neighborhood mosque, using books from Saudi Arabia!"

Of course, the other and more ominous manifestation of Islamization has been global terrorism, a phenomenon that will endure for years to come. The radical ideology espoused by al-Qa'ida and its leaders developed initially as a response to specific policies by Muslim states and by Western powers, especially the United States. After the withdrawal of the Soviet Union from Afghanistan, Usama Bin Ladin directed his violent campaign against the presence of U.S. "infidel" troops in Saudi Arabia, the "Land of the Two Sacred Mosques," and against Al Saud for inviting the U.S. military to stay in the country after Saddam Husayn was evicted from Kuwait in 1991. The perceived collusion between Al Saud and the United States became the cornerstone of Bin Ladin's deadly rhetoric, which has since expanded to include Palestine, Afghanistan, Iraq, Kashmir, Chechnya, and Indonesia. A Muslim Indonesian interlocutor sympathetic to Bin Ladin told me that U.S. "anti-Islamic" policy in Palestine, Iraq, and elsewhere is what drives the radicals' anti-American sentiment.

FACTORS CONTRIBUTING TO ISLAMIZATION

The factors that drive Islamic activism vary among activists and among countries, but it is possible to identify a few critical ones. The search for identity and the sense of defeat and injustice top the list of factors that Muslim interlocutors usually enumerate. Whether in Jordan, Egypt, or Indonesia, Muslim interlocutors have highlighted the importance of Islam as their identity anchor, especially as many of them do not feel a close allegiance toward the state. They also point to the "unjust wars" waged against Muslims and the ensuing defeats suffered by the Muslim *umma*. Other factors include regime repression, corruption, nepotism, and poor governance; economic and social stresses (e.g., unemployment, underemployment, poverty, discrimination, and alienation); Islamic education, especially at the elementary and high school levels; familial, personal, tribal, and other informal connections; and disenchantment with, and exclusion from, the political process. Beyond the individual level, other factors of Islamic activism include recruiting; resonance of the radical message and the role of the Internet in the globalization of jihad; state-supported *da'wa*; and ongoing territorial conflicts such as in Palestine, Iraq, Chechnya, Afghanistan, and Kashmir, which many Muslims perceive as Islamic conflicts.

Saudi proselytization in the past forty years has played a crucial role in spreading Islamic awareness among Muslims worldwide. The Saudis have spread *da'wa* through their funding of educational institutions, developmental projects, and international Islamic NGOs. Underlying this effort has been a pact that Al Saud had forged with the Wahhabi al-Shaykh family early in the twentieth century, which allowed Al Saud to rule Saudi Arabia as they see fit but designated the Wahhabi clerical establishment the moral guardian of Saudi Islam. Under this arrangement, Wahhabi Islam would govern the moral fabric of Saudi society and would underpin Saudi Arabia's international posture.

In the late 1960s the late King Faysal made Islamic *da'wa* a cardinal principle of Saudi foreign policy, with the aim of using Islam to fight communism and secular Arab nationalism, which at the time was spearheaded by Gamal Abd al-Nasir of Egypt. Faysal helped establish the Organization of the Islamic Conference and later on several international Islamic NGOs, beginning with the Muslim World League (MWL), or al-Rabita as it is known throughout the Muslim world, the International Islamic Relief Organization (IIRO), al-Haramayn, and the World Assembly of Muslim Youth. Saudi Arabia began to finance *da'wa* through these organizations and spread the Wahhabi interpretation of Islam. These NGOs, most of which are headquartered in Saudi Arabia and neighboring Gulf Arab countries, also offered scholarships to students in Muslim countries to study at Saudi Islamic universities, including the Imam Muhammad University in Riyadh, the Um al-Qura University in Mecca, and the Islamic University in Medina. Upon graduation, these students would go back to their countries to teach in Islamic schools and preach in mosques.

The Al Saud have taken another look at this type of proselytization and its inadvertent role in contributing to nurturing a violent jihadist mentality among the youth. Since the May 12, 2003, terrorist bombings in Saudi Arabia (which the Al Saud have described as their 9/11), the ruling family has reigned in extremist clerics, suggesting that the Al Saud understood that their homegrown radicals were threatening their internal stability as well as attracting unwelcome external attention. However, since the Iraq war and the ascendance of Shia power in that country at the expense of Sunnis, Saudi Arabia has tolerated, and in some cases financed, Sunni jihad in Iraq against the Shia.

I have visited numerous Qur'anic *madrasas* and other Islamic schools throughout the Muslim world financed by Saudi NGOs, especially MWL and IIRO. These NGOs also funded many mosques, libraries and printshops, and even agricultural programs. Most of the Qur'ans that are used in mosques in many Muslim countries are printed in Saudi Arabia and are distributed free of charge. An imam in Western Australia told me on a visit to his mosque he had to send quarterly reports about the mosque activities (programs, student enrollment, number of converts, etc.) to the Muslim World League office in Melbourne

and from there to the main office in Mecca. Several interlocutors in Malaysia, Albania, Uzbekistan, Tunisia, and Nigeria said
they either studied in Saudi universities or know of others who
have studied there. Traditionally, mainstream Muslim students
have studied at al-Azhar University in Cairo, the oldest functioning Islamic university in the world.

Right after the establishment of the Islamic Republic of Iran
in 1979, Saudi Arabia energized its *da'wa* efforts to combat the
proselytization activities of the Iranian supported Shia Ahl al-
Bayt NGO, in other parts of the Muslim world, especially in Africa. Because most Muslims are Sunnis and because of the largesse of Saudi money, Iranian-supported Shia proselytization
did not take root and diminished significantly by the end of the
1990s. Nigeria is a case in point. From the mid-1980s to the
mid-1990s, Iranian influence spread rapidly in the northern
part of the country through the Iranian-supported Zakzaki
group. However, by the late 1990s, Zakzaki lost influence, and
Saudi-supported conservative Sunni ideology became dominant, including among high school and college students. One
could see the IIRO logo displayed in numerous villages and
towns across the Nigerian landscape in the north. Saudi NGOs
also provided free food during the month of Ramadan, drilled
wells for agricultural projects, and distributed food and other
assistance to needy families during 'Id al-Fitr and 'Id al-Adha,
Sunni Islam's two most important religious feasts.

In the past half decade, however, several government officials
in Arab and non-Arab Muslim majority and Muslim minority
countries—for example, Albania, Macedonia, Bosnia, Tunisia,
Kenya, Uzbekistan, Turkmenistan, Singapore, Thailand, India,
and Indonesia—told me of their concern about the pervasive
Wahhabi-Salafi influence among their Muslim communities. To
combat this trend, these officials began to send students to study
Islam at universities, including in Turkey, Malaysia, Jordan, Morocco, and Egypt, which they considered more "open-minded"
than Saudi universities. Some of these officials admitted, however, that, once their students leave the country, they have no
way of monitoring their foreign travel, unless they study abroad
on government scholarship; students who finance their own

education are generally beyond government supervision. In addition to Saudi-financed education, officials in these countries also complained about the Salafi proselytization through Saudi-funded religious satellite television stations such as 'Iqra'. The curriculum at Saudi universities is saturated with courses in Arabic language and literature, Islamic history, jurisprudence, Hadith, and philosophy, and when students graduate with a concentration in these subjects, they find themselves unqualified to compete for jobs in the modern economy. Many of them become unemployed, continue to live at home, and are unable to get married and have their own home. They become frustrated, angry, and develop low self-esteem. The only jobs available to many of them are teaching in Islamic schools and preaching. A highly successful Saudi industrialist told me that when the Saudi government ordered businesses to "Saudize" the labor force, that is, to hire Saudis rather than expatriates, he personally reviewed resumes of applicants and to his dismay discovered that "only one in a hundred was qualified to work in his businesses."

EDUCATION AND ISLAMIZATION

Education is a key factor in the growth of Islamization. Grade school and high school textbooks in the Arab world and other Muslim countries are replete with Islamic references and play a major role in socializing young children into a certain vision of Islam and of Islam's relations with non-Muslims. Textbooks in selected Arab countries inculcate schoolchildren with an Islamic worldview strongly grounded in the Qur'an and the traditions of the Prophet Muhammad and the first four "rightly guided" caliphs after him. Although the books vary from one country to the next—with Saudi Arabia the most conservative and Morocco the least—they exhibit common characteristics. First, Islamic teachings—whether the Wahhabi doctrine in Saudi Arabia or al-Azhar teachings in Egypt—are presented in the textbooks as infallible sources of individual behavior, human interaction, and relations between Muslims and non-Muslims. Second, the textbooks identify the enemies of Islam and the Arabs as the Jews, for "deception against the Prophet" in Medina in the seventh century and their "occupation of Jerusalem" today; Christian "Crusaders"; Western colonialism; and Zionism. Third, the textbooks teach that Islam underpins all learning and the pursuit of knowledge, whether in history, philosophy, the sciences, or Arabic language and literature; that Islam is the source of political legitimacy; and that Islamic concepts of consultation (*shura*) and allegiance (*bay'a*) form the basis of good governance.

High school social studies textbooks in some of these countries, much like grade school books, teach students that Islam, Arab nationalism, patriotism, and the struggle of the Palestinian people are inexorably linked. Regardless of the peace treaties and economic and security arrangements some of these states, especially Egypt and Jordan, have signed with Israel, the textbooks do not recognize the existence of the Jewish state, do not show it on their geography maps, and view the establishment of Israel as an unjust usurpation of Arab lands. The textbooks present Arab high school students with a static picture of society based on the Qur'an and the Prophet Muhammad's experiences in seventh-century Arabia and do not encourage any debate of the revealed word or the traditions of the Prophet. It is as if the door of reasoning (*ijtihad*), once open to different interpretations of Islamic dogma, has been permanently closed, and neither regimes nor the religious establishment (*'ulama*) wishes to see it open.

Arab youths inculcated with ideas from these textbooks face an almost irreconcilable dichotomy between the traditional teachings of Islam as presented in the textbooks and the onslaught of new ideas emanating from globalization, satellite television, the Internet, political and economic reform movements, and worldwide impulses toward democratization. A survey of selected textbooks leads one to conclude that a curriculum grounded in a rigid interpretation of Islam in societies desperately striving for economic progress and in the midst of continued sectarian violence among Muslims and between Muslims and the West paves the way for violent confrontations between Muslim youth and the perceived enemies of Islam. In nations rife with increasing unemployment and a deepening gap between rich and poor—in an environment of regime neglect, corruption, and repression—these textbooks will inevitably push some segments of the rising generation to become radicalized and susceptible to Bin Ladin's message that the United States is the enemy of Islam.

In response to domestic and international demands for reform, Arab regimes began to talk about reform in areas like economics and education, but a wide gap remains between words and deeds. Educational reform in some countries has resulted in the introduction of more "modern" subjects in the curriculum and teacher training, but to address the narrow mind-set taught in some of these textbooks, the content of the textbooks must be revised toward promoting pluralism and inclusiveness and a more tolerant view of other religions and ethnic groups. Arab reformers continue to hammer on the theme of educational reform, and Arab regimes continue to talk the talk of reform. However, as the religious establishment—al-Azhar 'ulama in Egypt and Salafi-Wahhabi clerics in Saudi Arabia—control the curriculum and have the final say on the content of government textbooks, pro-reform bureaucrats in ministries of education face an uphill battle in curricular reform. When I asked a senior education ministry official in a Gulf Arab country about the status of textbook reform, he said, "We are proceeding on the path of reform, and inshallah [God willing] we will get there soon." When I related this exchange to a secular, pro-reform liberal thinker in the same country, he quipped, "inshallah reminds him of the Spanish word mañana but doesn't have the same sense of urgency!"

It should be pointed out however that several Arab states have embarked on major projects to revise their textbooks by replacing previous Qur'anic citations with others that are less exclusive and more tolerant. Recent textbook editions, especially in the United Arab Emirates, Saudi Arabia, and Egypt, reflect some of the revisions. It is interesting to note, however, that the geography textbooks, even the new editions, in several of these countries still omit Israel from their maps of the Middle East and show "Palestine" covering the land between the Jordan

River and the Mediterranean Sea. Saudi textbooks, understandably, continue to espouse the Wahhabi interpretation of Islam,
which tends to encourage Muslims to eschew relations with
non-Muslims.

SHIA ACTIVISM

Much of our discussion of Islamization thus far applies to Sunni
Islam; in recent years, however, Shia activism has become more
pronounced in the Middle East. The defeat of Saddam Husayn
and the Sunni regime in Iraq and the rise of Shia political power
in that country have empowered the Shia not only in Iraq but
across the greater Middle East. The "Arc of Shia resurgence," as
some Sunni Arab leaders have described it, stretches from Lebanon to Pakistan and cuts across Iraq, Bahrain, Kuwait, Saudi
Arabia, the United Arab Emirates, and Afghanistan. Although
they constitute 10 to 15 percent of the 1.4 billion Muslims
worldwide, the Shia in recent centuries have controlled only one
country, Iran. Iraq became the second country to come under
Shia control. The parliamentary elections in Bahrain in November 2006, where the Shia are also a majority of the population,
resulted in the Shia bloc al-Wifaq winning seventeen seats in
the forty-seat lower house of the national legislature. Al-Wifaq
boycotted the 2002 election but was urged to participate in this
election by Shia religious leaders, including Grand Ayatollah Ali
al-Husayni Sistani. The two Sunni groups (the Muslim Brotherhood and the Salafis), which were supported by the al-Khalifa
Sunni ruling family, won a total of twelve seats. The Shia success
at the polls occurred despite some election irregularities and the
bussing in of recently naturalized Sunni citizens to polling
places. Shia critics described this attempt by the government as
"political citizenship" designed to alter the demographic com-
position of the country, according to media reports. The election results offer another example of the continuing Islamization of Arab politics and of the rising Shia political power. It is
interesting to note that the pro-democracy secular, nationalist
action group did not win even one seat. A Shia parliamentarian
in Bahrain said after the election, "If free elections are held any-

where in the Middle East, Islamic groups would win." Votes in Bahrain were cast principally along sectarian lines, a distressing phenomenon that is becoming more apparent in Arab politics since the invasion of Iraq. The election was another indication of the rising political power of the Shia as a voice for democracy in Sunni-controlled states.

Shia political leaders across the region have concluded that the democratic process could be an effective tool to lead them to power, either as a majority (Iraq and Bahrain) or as influential minorities (Lebanon, Saudi Arabia, Kuwait, and elsewhere). These leaders have emerged as the most vocal advocates of democracy, a fact that has alarmed many Sunni authoritarian regimes. Shia political leaders in Iraq and Bahrain have also learned that their overt commitment to democracy finds resonance in the West. American policymakers have initially endorsed the newly articulated Shia democracy platform in the belief that it would be inclusive and pluralistic; however, this endorsement cooled off considerably once they realized that Shia democracy in Iraq began to systematically exclude Sunnis from the post-Saddam political order and deny them access to economic opportunity and political power.

Shia political revival as a result of Iraq, Hizballah's ability to survive Israel's military assault on Lebanon in the summer of 2006, and a resurgence of Iran as a key regional power have alarmed many Sunni Muslims and leaders in the region, especially as some of these leaders have hitched their wagon to the United States. More and more statements and declarations by Sunni Muslims, moderate thinkers and radical clerics alike, have been published denouncing the "sectarian killings" of Sunnis in Iraq and growing Shia proselytization (*tashayyuʿ* or Shiafication) in Sunni communities, including in Egypt, Sudan, Yemen, and elsewhere. For the first time in centuries, Shia political activism is being conducted in the forefront of Middle East politics without being afraid of repression by the Sunni majority, resulting in new debates, a deepening divide between Islam's two primary sects, and potential conflicts within Islam. Several examples illustrate the growing rift between Sunnis and Shia and the increasing vitriol by Sunni groups and clerics against the Shia. A Saudi religious scholar who teaches Islamic studies at the King Saud University sent a letter to the al-Azhar University in Cairo on April 19, 2007, urging the *ulama* in that institution to realize the dangers of growing "Shia penetration" in Egypt and the resulting threats of social and sectarian conflicts. A violent Sunni-Shia altercation occurred at the Cairo Book Exhibit on February 1, 2007, which reflected the growing anger among some Sunnis about the perceived "Shiafication" in Sunni communities. The Sudanese Supreme Council of Muslim Groups—which includes Ansar al-Sunna, the Muslim Brotherhood, and other Sunni organizations—warned the Sudanese government and people on December 6, 2006, against the active "Shiafication" efforts by Shia proselytizers in Sudan. The Supreme Council accused Iran of driving and financing this effort and claimed that whole villages have adopted Shia Islam and that Shia mosques and prayer places have spread all over Khartoum. The council's statement described the Shia as not true Muslims and "rejectionists" or *rafida* and demanded the government ban Shia books from entering the country.

Shaykh Yusif al-Qaradawi in interviews with *al-Masri al-Yaym* newspaper in Egypt on November 27, 2006 and September 9, 2008, stated that he supported Hizballah in its struggle against Israel but opposed Hizballah's and other Shia groups' efforts to spread the Shia doctrine among Sunnis. On December 10, 2006, thirty-eight prominent Saudi clerics published a statement decrying the "massacres" and "sectarian cleansing" perpetrated by Iraqi Shia against the Sunnis in that country. The statement called on Sunni Muslims worldwide to support Iraqi Sunnis, renounce the "atrocities" committed against them, and "wake up" to the dangers of the Shia "plots and conspiracies" against the "Muslim *umma*" and said, "We should openly side with our Sunni brothers in Iraq and lend them all appropriate forms of support." The statement, which presumably would not have been published without Saudi government implicit approval, claimed Shia militias were "killing Sunnis with Iranian and U.S. support." The statement frequently referred to what it called a "Crusader, Safavi, *rafidi* (rejectionist)" conspiracy—that is, the United States, Iran, and the Shia—and implied that Iraq currently is under a dual occupation by the United States and Iran. Among the signatories of the statement are Shaykh Abd al-Rahman bin Nasir al-Barrak, Shaykh Safar al-Hawali, Shaykh Nasir al-Umar, Shaykh Ali al-Ghamdi, Shaykh Muhammad al-Qahtani, and Shaykh Salman al-Awda. Two days after the publication of the Saudi statement, Shaykh al-Barrak, the first cleric to sign the Saudi statement, issued a separate and a more extreme and vicious *fatwa* against the Shia. He accused the Shia of duplicity, conniving, and deception and said that "because of their false religion, they are more dangerous to Muslims than Jews and Christians." He concluded by saying that "the Sunni and Shia *mathhabs* (beliefs) are completely contradictory and cannot be reconciled; the talk of Sunni-Shia rapprochement is utterly false."

The ongoing sectarian debate within Islam, especially among Muslim intellectuals from both sects, has revolved around the following key questions: Will Sunni-Shia sectarian violence spread to Iraq's neighboring states and how will Sunni Arab and non-Arab states—for example, Saudi Arabia, Egypt, Jordan, and Pakistan—respond to potential sectarian violence and *fitna* in their societies as a result of growing Shia political assertiveness? What role will Sunni and Shia thinkers play in toning down sectarian vitriol and push for sectarian rapprochement over the next five years? Beyond domestic sectarian violence, will the region witness the formation of new regional alignments driven by Sunni-Shia sectarianism and Arab-Persian tensions reflecting a sense of "Sunni solidarity" and Shia assertiveness? Will such alignments enable conservative Saudi radical Salafi clerics to preach to their followers a new "jihad" against their Shia coreligionists? And will this type of violence lead to a Saudi-Iranian confrontation? Although the summer 2006 Lebanon war enhanced Hizballah's prestige as an Arab "resistance" or *muqawama* movement against Israel, will increased Sunni-Shia conflicts push Sunni Arab nationalists to alter their view of Hizballah, perceiving it instead as a conduit for Shia Iran? Finally, what implications will these developments have for the United States and its standing and influence in the region as well as for Israel? Middle East analysts generally agree that Iran is not interested in fomenting sectarian violence in the region because an unstable Middle East would not serve Iran's strategic interests. The military support that certain elements within the Iranian regime have been providing the insurgency in Iraq aims at forcing the United States to terminate its occupation because America's massive military presence in Iraq and throughout the Persian Gulf and the Arabian Sea is not comforting to the leaders in Tehran. Similarly, Iran's support of Hizballah in Lebanon is another extension of Iran's pursuit of its regional geopolitical interests. Most analysts equally agree that Iran's approach to foreign policy seems to reflect a sense of pragmatism rather than a strict adherence to Shia theology or religious ideology. This argument might also explain Iran's support of some Sunni "resistance" or jihadist groups despite its opposition to the global millenarian radical Sunni ideology of al-Qaʿida.

Islamic Political Party Politics

The frequent participation of Islamic political parties across the Muslim world in national legislative elections and their behavior after being elected are indicators of their commitment to the democratic process and their pragmatic approach to politics and political change. None of those parties, either during the electoral campaign or after being elected, has demanded that their Islamic ideology dominate the political system or that *Sharia* be installed as the source of legislation in their respective countries. When I asked representatives of these parties over the years about their electoral strategies and how they reconciled their Islamic ideology with a Western brand of secular democracy, they frequently made three central points to buttress their position: first, Islam is not inimical to democracy ("Islamic dictators are," a Muslim contact told me); second, they do not intend to use the democratic process to install *Sharia* by force or through clever parliamentary maneuverings ("if the majority of the people decides to opt for *Sharia*, they would support it but will not spearhead a movement on behalf of *Sharia*," another interlocutor told me); and, third, these parties should be judged by their performance in national legislatures, not by their ideology. A Western-educated Muslim activist asked, "Why is it okay for you to judge Christian and other ideological political parties by their performance as compared to their official ideology but it's not okay to do the same with Islamic parties?" Analysis of the behavior of some of these parties, whether they are a majority in the national legislature as in the case of AKP in Turkey or Hamas in Palestine or a minority in national legislatures as in the case of several Islamic political parties (Hizballah in Lebanon, the Muslim Brotherhood in Egypt, the Islamic Party of Malaysia, Prosperous Justice Party in Indonesia, Justice and Development in Morocco, the Islamic Constitutional Movement in Kuwait, and al-Wifaq in Bahrain), indicates that these parties engage in legislative processes like other so-called secular political parties, compromise over the passage of bills, and for the most part focus on bread-and-butter issues that are of concern to their constituents. As a Hamas parliamentarian once said, "We are too busy focusing on providing jobs, electricity, home cooking fuel, travel permits, and garbage collection and have no time to promote *Sharia*." However, party activists in several countries indicated they viewed *Sharia* as the moral underpinning of society and a guide for individual and group behavior. A Muslim Brotherhood member in Egypt told me that most of the issues his organization raises in and out of parliament are not "really Islamic." He said they have articulated an agenda of issues that transcend the "Islamic street," including the end to corruption, regime repression, and violations of human rights; freedoms of speech, assembly, and organization; solutions to unemployment and poverty; and social and public services. He added these and other issues of "poor governance" will occupy Islamic parties for years to come.

Legislative elections in recent years in Palestinian territories, Egypt, Iraq, Lebanon, Malaysia, Indonesia, Morocco, and Bahrain and municipal elections in Saudi Arabia clearly indicate that Islamic political groups and parties are moving aggressively toward political participation regardless of the nature of the regime. Contrast this with the position that some of these groups took in the early 1990s against participating in politics because of what they saw then as the "un-Islamic" behavior of some regimes. In the Arab world, Islamic political parties and groups are already serving in national legislatures in Kuwait, Yemen, Jordan, Bahrain, Lebanon, Iraq, and Morocco. In the wider Islamic world, Islamic parties are actively involved in the political process in Turkey, Sudan, Pakistan, Bangladesh, Malaysia, and Indonesia. Shia political groups, as was pointed out, have also expanded their political participation in Iraq, Lebanon, Kuwait, and Bahrain. Of course, the establishment of the Islamic Republic of Iran in 1979 created the first Shia dominated government in the region in centuries.

Among the reasons that have contributed to the electoral success of Islamic groups are the failure of secular nationalist elites to organize politically around themes that appeal to the electorate and their ideological marginalization because of their association with discredited ruling regimes. These elites have in recent decades joined forces with authoritarian governments, whether military, civilian, or dynastic; benefited from access to the economic largesse of the state; and, in turn, acquiesced in many of the top-down policies designed to preserve authoritarian regime rule. Consequently, these elites, like many of the regimes they have supported, have lost their legitimacy, and when the political space provided an opening, though narrow and highly prescribed, Islamic parties became more appealing to the average voter. A Turkish Muslim activist admitted to me in a conversation in the mid-1990s that the Refah Islamic Party received many votes that were cast against the corruption, mismanagement, and poor economic policies of the ruling party. So was the case with voters in Palestine, where many of the ballots cast for Hamas reflected the voters' anger against the corruption, mismanagement, and nepotism of the Palestinian Authority that was installed as part of the Oslo Accords in 1993.

The weakening of the Middle Eastern state and its inability to provide for the well-being of its citizens in the past two decades have also contributed to the success of Islamic parties at the polls. As the Arab Islamic electorate becomes more critical of U.S. policy in the greater Middle East and of Arab and Muslim regimes' support of this policy—whether toward Iraq, Iran, or Palestine—popular anger has often translated into votes for Islamic parties. Finally, the Hamas electoral victory in Palestine and the ensuing U.S. refusal to engage the Hamas-led government have inadvertently strengthened Islamic parties' claim that they are the new democrats in the region. It is important to note that much diversity characterizes the rise and electoral successes of these groups. Leadership, local conditions in each country, indigenous agendas, and the regional and international political, security, and economic contexts have influenced the electoral behavior and success of Islamic political parties and groups at the ballot box. These groups, whether in Baghdad, Gaza, or Kuala Lumpur, are heavily attuned to their local conditions and experiences and are charting a postelection course that reflects these experiences.

To summarize, the history of Islamic political parties in the Middle East region in the past half century is replete with sloganeering about the need to establish a *Sharia*-based society predicated on Islamic values, social mores, and theological guidelines. However, once these parties became part of the political process, they competed for votes, moderated their message, cooperated with other, mostly secular groups to pass legislation, and generally adopted a pragmatic attitude toward governance. In two recent parliamentary elections, Muslim Brotherhood candidates ran as "independent" under the "Islam is the solution" platform. The "parties of God" have at long last decided to set aside their commitment to "divine rule" (*hukm*) and play in the sandbox of the "democracy of man"—a strategic shift that mainstream Muslims have strongly endorsed and radical Muslims violently rejected. Arab and Muslim regimes have yet to comprehend this shift, embrace it, and exploit it in the furtherance of genuine political reform and democratization in the region.

ISLAMIC ACTIVISM, CIA BRIEFINGS, AND U.S. POLICY RESPONSES

The Central Intelligence Agency and other entities in the U.S. intelligence community became aware of the emerging trends of political activism and the Islamization of Middle Eastern politics almost two decades ago and frequently briefed these trends to senior policymakers. In the past two decades, but especially since September 11, 2001, several senior analysts and I participated in a series of briefings designed to inform senior policymakers in the executive and legislative branches on the rise of Islamic activism, the meaning and implications of these trends, and the long-term trajectory of this phenomenon. As the book points out, reaching out to the Muslim world should include strategies for engaging mainstream Islamic political parties and groups and reestablishing formal contacts with the Egyptian Muslim Brotherhood that were halted in the late 1990s in response to objections from the Egyptian government. The Directorate of Intelligence provided its analysis of political Islam and the growing phenomenon of Islamic activism to policymakers through articles in the President's Daily Brief (PDB), strategic papers, trip reports, responses to inquiries or taskings from policymakers, and high-level briefings (which I provided on several occasions). The Directorate of Intelligence had also organized annual academic meetings for U.S. government analysts and managers from the intelligence and policy communities to explore different facets—legal, economic, cultural, educational, religious—of Islamic activism.

The analysis we provided focused on a few key topics, including the rise of political activism across the Muslim world; the differences among the various forms of activism; the thinkers of the different movements, both moderate and radical; the changing ideologies of the various parties and groups; the political landscape in different political, cultural, economic, and social environments in which Islamic political parties have operated; and the historical underpinnings of some of these developments. We also briefed on Islamic civil society institutions and their role in promoting Islamic activism, debates within Islam about the future direction of the faith, and the role of education in various Muslim countries and its role in nurturing a particular worldview among Muslim youth. Briefings and analytic products highlighted three key aspects for policymakers: first, there is no such a thing as one Islamic world, one Islamic "street," or one Islamic society, but there are many; second, much of the

Islamic activism we observed was a benign form of political involvement and not a threat to the West or to the United States, but that the threat came from a small minority that was bent on radicalism and potential conflict with the non-Muslim world; and, third, much of the activism focused on domestic agendas, whether in Egypt or Malaysia, and was not connected to or driven by global Islamic activism, jihad, or terrorism. The intelligence community, having nurtured over the years a deep expertise in Muslim societies, cultures, historical experiences, and languages, offered senior policymakers a wealth of information in this area on a regular basis. After 9/11, our briefings and other analytic products divided Islamic activism into two broad categories: a small percentage of Islamic activists who preach a radical agenda and engaged in terrorism; and a vast majority of activists who advocate gradual change through existing political systems and who have adopted a pragmatic approach to politics. We roughly estimated the first group at 1–2 percent; the other at 98–99 percent. The greatest challenge the United States faces is how to reach out to the vast majority of Muslims while relentlessly pursuing those who commit acts of terror.

Unfortunately, before 9/11 senior policymakers did not show much interest in the topic beyond focusing on specific terrorist acts and unilateral relations with Muslim states. Although right after 9/11 the country understandably focused heavily on terrorism and the terrorists, in subsequent years the focus has changed very little. In senior-level briefings CIA analysts gave at the White House, to the National Security Council (NSC), and to Senate and House leaders, especially members of the intelligence committees, we tried to point out the complexity and diversity that characterize the Islamic world and the ongoing debate between the large moderate majority of Muslims and the small minority of radicals. We also briefed senior officials at the NSC and at the State Department on the results of trips we took to Muslims countries and numerous meetings we had with Muslim interlocutors and explained that, according to these interviews, many Muslim activists were committed to political reform and peaceful change through democratization and were seriously interested in engaging the United States on issues of governance. We cited examples from Egypt, Jordan, Syria, Palestine, Turkey, South Asia, Southeast Asia, Central Asia, and the Balkans where Muslim activists were eager to meet with official and unofficial U.S. visitors and engage them in conversations about democracy. Some Islamic party activists have urged the United States to deal with them directly as potential democrats and not be "duped" by the antidemocratic rhetoric of authoritarian regimes who viewed all Islamic activists as potential terrorists and a threat to regime and, by extension, U.S. security. A Muslim activist in Uzbekistan told me that the Karimov regime views all Muslim oppositionists as "Salafi Wahhabis," not to be trusted. When an Uzbek official was asked to define what he meant by "Salafi Wahhabis," he could not. The United States had urged several Arab and Muslim countries to move toward democracy and political reform and make their political systems more inclusive, but they ignored these calls and did not alter their repressive and antidemocratic practices. Security has clearly trumped democracy, and U.S.-Muslim world engagement remains elusive.

Chapter 2

INTELLIGENCE, POLITICAL ISLAM, AND POLICYMAKERS

IN THE PAST TWO DECADES, the Intelligence Community, especially the Central Intelligence Agency, has analyzed and reported on rising trends in political Islam and Islamic radicalism and the potential challenges they could pose to the United States. The CIA, especially its Directorate of Intelligence, began to dedicate resources and personnel to the development of substantive expertise in political Islam and to brief policymakers regularly and frequently on this phenomenon. In the late 1980s and early 1990s, policymakers for the most part did not pay much attention to rising Islamic activism, but after September 11, 2001, they came to view Islamic activism through the prism of terrorism. By focusing on the terrorists, a tiny but lethal minority of Muslims worldwide, policymakers in Western countries ignored the rising trends of Islamization among the vast majority of Muslims and arguably gave the impression that their dealings with Muslims were to be pursued primarily through the so-called global war on terror. Statements by some policymakers, especially at the U.S. Department of State, during this period that America had no quarrel with Islam were not matched by actions on the ground. Nor did these policymakers offer tangible programs or cultivate new relationships to convince Muslims of the veracity of their position. This chapter highlights the CIA's efforts to expand its expertise in political Islam and its attempts to educate senior policymakers on the "Islamic awakening," the Islamization of Muslim societies, and the diversity and complexity of global Islam. The chapter also shows that some policymakers did not take a nuanced approach toward Islamic activism; the growing interest of Muslim thinkers and political parties to participate in the political process; or Muslim aspirations, interests, and ideologies.

INTELLIGENCE AND POLICY: ROOTS OF TENSION

Dating back to the late 1980s, the Central Intelligence Agency recognized the threat of terrorism to the United States, vigorously pursued terrorists worldwide, and frequently disrupted many of their plots. Similarly, the CIA briefed the administration on the larger cultural context in which terrorists emerge and operate and the factors that would make this context less hospitable to terrorists. The specific political Islam topics on which I and other CIA analysts briefed policymakers in the past two decades included the rise of Islamic activism; the meaning and implications of these trends; the cultural, economic, leadership, political, and social context of Islamic activism; the Islamization of Arab and Muslim politics; the complexity and diversity of the Muslim world; the rise of radicalism and the ensuing debates between radical and moderate thinkers; the expanding role and funding of Islamic NGOs and charitable societies worldwide; and the growth of Islamic political parties, the indigenous agendas they espouse, their strategic shift toward participatory democracy, and the challenge they pose to pro-U.S. authoritarian Muslim regimes in the Middle East and elsewhere. The intelligence community sought to offer senior policymakers a wealth of information in this area on a regular basis.

During this period, the CIA offered policymakers a variety of products focusing on political Islam, including National Intelligence Estimates, special reports, strategic analysis assessments, short research papers, field assessments usually written by senior CIA representatives in different countries (known in the agency as Aardwolves), TDY trip reports, analytic reports from academic conferences, the President's Daily Brief (PDB), oral high-level briefings, and analytic reports of pronouncements and audio and video messages by Usama Bin Ladin and other top al-Qaʿida leaders. Since September 11, 2001, CIA analysts have also responded to thousands of questions or taskings from senior policymakers dealing with every imaginable aspect of political Islam. The subjects of these taskings included, among other things, the meaning of specific key dates in the Islamic calendar, especially the month of Ramadan; Arabic or Islamic words and phrases; Sunni-Shia doctrinal differences; the legal schools of Sunni Islam, the Twelvers' Shia ideology and the history of the Imamate, and Sufism; the nature and different meanings of jihad and "martyrdom"; millenarian thought in Islam; the growing debates within Islam about which vision of Islam Muslims should pursue; the process of radicalization; Islamic education and textbooks; global Islamic proselytization or da'wa; traditional Islamic reformist schools and thinkers; and the influential role of al-Azhar and other Islamic universities on proselytization and radicalization, and the differences and similarities between these universities.

Policymaker queries also covered the role of Saudi Arabia and Saudi universities and NGOs in spreading Wahhabi Islam throughout the world, the teachings of Wahhabi and Salafi Islam, specific chapters or *suras* in the Qur'an and their applicability to, and misuse by, radical jihadists, the history and ideology of the Muslim Brotherhood and its influence on Sunni political groups and political parties in the Muslim world, and the "dos and don'ts" that American policymakers should observe in their dealings with Muslim leaders. CIA analysts provided senior policymakers with lists of Islamic terms and phrases and their nuanced use by Islamic activists and jihadists and indicated what terms would or would not resonate well with Muslim audiences. The claim made by some neo-cons in the nation's capital such as Richard Perle (2007) that the CIA failed "to understand and sound an alarm at the rise of jihadist fundamentalism" is patently false. Perle obviously either was not privy to or decided to ignore the myriad briefings given to senior policymakers and their senior staff. Clearly, information and intelligence analysis and judgments about political Islam were transmitted to the executive and legislative branches on a regular basis.

As the CIA's senior analyst on Islamic activism from the early 1990s to mid-2006, when I retired, I helped develop and nurture the agency's expertise on Islam. I was also involved on a

regular basis in briefing senior policymakers on Islamic issues
and developments. Oftentimes, I would be tasked by name to
respond to specific questions on Islam from senior officials at
the White House, the National Security Council, the Department of State, the Department of Defense, the Department of
Homeland Security, and the U.S. Congress. In the summer and
early fall of 2004, I participated, with White House approval, in
briefing the Democratic presidential and vice-presidential candidates on Islamic activism and radicalization and on exploring
creative ways to engage the Muslim world. The individuals I
briefed were generally interested in the topic, asked probing
questions, and explored ways to reach out to mainstream Muslims worldwide beyond the realm of terrorism.

POLITICS TRUMPS NATIONAL SECURITY

As has been reported in the media, Professor Tariq Ramadan (a
Swiss-born Islamic scholar and the grandson of Hasan al-Banna,
the founder of the Egyptian Muslim Brotherhood) had accepted
a teaching position at the University of Notre Dame in Indiana
to begin in the fall of 2004. He was granted a U.S. visa, made the
necessary travel, housing, and school plans for him and his family, and was ready to travel to the United States. Less than a
month before his travel was to commence, however, he was informed by the U.S. Embassy in Switzerland that his visa was
revoked, which, he was told, was for national security reasons.
American academic organizations protested the revocation in
letters sent to the secretary of state and the secretary of homeland security. According to numerous media reports in the
summer and fall of 2004, after a further review of the Ramadan
file, the State Department decided to rescind the visa revocation
and asked Professor Ramadan to reapply for a visa, which he
did. Many academics and media writers argued at the time that
Ramadan's visa was revoked for political, not security reasons.

Despite protests from Notre Dame and other academic institutions and professional associations, Ramadan could not get
his visa in time. As one academic familiar with Notre Dame told
me at the time, "Notre Dame is not in the business of hiring

radicals to teach its students and was convinced of Ramadan's scholarly credentials and moderate views on Muslim-Christian relations." By the time he was informed of the State Department's decision to rescind the revocation of his visa, it was already halfway in the fall semester and too late for him to make new travel arrangements, and he decided against pursuing the teaching position at Notre Dame. It is interesting to note that following the Notre Dame incident, Ramadan was appointed an adviser to then British prime minister Tony Blair.

This case is instructive in that many Western and Muslim scholars generally viewed Ramadan as a moderate Islamic thinker who could be a bridge between the West and the Muslim world. Ramadan, like a few other Islamic thinkers in the United States and Europe, is engaged in a new reasoning or *ijtihad*, which would help Muslims reconcile their faith with their citizenship in Western countries. As a practicing Muslim, Ramadan has argued that the Qur'an, revealed to Muhammad in seventh-century Arabia, should be read and understood in the context of a twenty-first-century globalized world. Of course, Ramadan, like other modernizing thinkers, had made statements in other contexts that were critical of American foreign policy, but on the whole, in the context of the great divide between radicalism and moderation, people like Tariq Ramadan could play a positive role in promoting a dialogue of religions, not a clash of civilizations. Reaching out to people like him would give the United States new and much needed inroads into the world of Islam. Ramadan's case became a cause célèbre throughout the Muslim world, especially among the educated elites who judged American calls for dialogue with Muslims, in light of the Ramadan case, as hollow and insincere.

Building Expertise

Beginning in the early 1990s, the CIA, through its Directorate of Intelligence, embarked on a systematic effort to deepen its analysts' expertise in political Islam through a commitment in resources and personnel. Although initially minimal, the commitment signaled the agency's interest in this subject and its

realization that the issue would grow and become more critical
to U.S. national security. Furthermore, the CIA was the only
U.S. government entity to exhibit such a commitment to building expertise in political Islam. Initially, the CIA did not approach political Islam from a global perspective but focused on
it in the context of the Middle East, which was viewed at the
time as the "heartland" of Islam. The Directorate of Intelligence
hired me as a scholar in residence and empowered me to deepen
the Directorate's analytic expertise on political Islam. I was in-
structed to develop a robust outreach program to academic experts in Islamic studies and cultures, establish a training program for analysts interested in the subject, travel to Muslim
countries and engage Muslim interlocutors, and produce analytic products that U.S. government officials could use in dealing with political Islam questions.

Following the end of the Cold War and the collapse of the
Soviet Union, several new states that had nominally Muslim
majorities emerged in Central Asia and the Balkans, and signs
of Islamic activism—as evidenced in the growth of Islamic
NGOs, political parties, nonstate units, religious recordings,
and Qur'anic schools—became visible throughout the Muslim
world. Algeria was a case in point. The Islamic Salvation Front
became a critical player in Algerian elections and won the vote
in December 1991. In reaction, the military staged a coup in
January 1992 and canceled the next round of elections, paving
the way for a bloody civil war that claimed hundreds of thousands of casualties. The American government at the time was
sympathetic to the Algerian military's decision to quash the
elections, and senior American policymakers argued that an Islamic victory would have empowered Islamic activists to form
an Islamic, and presumably antidemocratic, government. Former assistant secretary of state Edward Djerejian said in a public speech at the Meridian House in Washington, D.C., in 1992
that the United States was concerned that Islamic activists would
use the elections to come to power and then cancel future elections through the "one man, one vote, one time" rule. Of course,
no one knows what the Front would have done had it come to
power; it was not given the chance. Other Islamic activist move-

ments began to challenge existing regimes in the early 1990s in Saudi Arabia, Egypt, Turkey, Yemen, and elsewhere.

The collapse of the Suharto regime in Indonesia paved the way for Islamic parties to enter the political process, and in Turkey the Islamic Refah Party won an impressive plurality of the vote in national elections. Bin Ladin and other Islamic radicals called on the Saudi government to remove American and other "infidel" soldiers from Arabia. Arab *mujahidin* and other Islamic activists who fought against the Soviet military in Afghanistan returned to their countries with a shared jihadist experience and a euphoric feeling of "victory" against a superpower. Regimes that encouraged their young men to go and do jihad in Afghanistan began to reap what they sowed as militant jihadists began to question the legitimacy and "un-Islamic" behavior of the same regimes that sent them to Afghanistan in the first place. An "Islamic awakening," (alternately known as the "Islamic current" or the "Islamic trend") began to crystallize in Muslim countries demanding a say in the affairs of state, which would have long-term implications for Muslim regimes, for Muslim–non-Muslim relations, and for the United States. That was the impetus that drove the CIA and the intelligence community to view the rise of Islamic activism as the first post–Cold War challenge to the international order.

ACADEMIC OUTREACH

In order to benefit from the wealth of knowledge that exists in academia on Islamic activism and on Muslim societies in general, the CIA encouraged me to put in place a comprehensive academic outreach program and urged its analysts to stay current on the open-source literature and academic research and publications. Although the CIA academic outreach had a rocky start in the early 1990s—academics were rather skittish in dealing with the world of intelligence—in the following decade and a half the program became robust and acquired credibility in the world of academe. I systematically reached out to academics and other private-sector experts on the subject and began to invite them to annual conferences and monthly symposia series. CIA analysts at the time were not comfortable engaging the private sector and seeking information through what the CIA calls "open source." My professional reputation in the academic community encouraged academics to participate in these conferences as they quickly realized that we in the intelligence community were interested in learning from them, not in censuring their views or prescribing what topics they could or could not discuss. Senior academics who participated in the first two conferences began to strongly encourage other, and perhaps more skeptical, professors to participate in the CIA-sponsored outreach program because of its quality. One senior professor told a colleague of his, "Don't worry about participating in the program; I know the organizer and the quality of the program."

The annual conferences focused on topics that were at the forefront of academic research regarding the Middle East and the Islamic world, including Islamic activism, the "Islamic awakening," civil society institutions in Muslim countries, governance and authoritarian regimes, Islamic political parties, Islamic economics, demography, education, public opinion in Muslim countries, ruling elites, and political reform and democratization. The annual conferences, occasional workshops, and monthly symposia approached these topics thematically and from the perspectives of individual countries using a comparative, interdisciplinary approach. The purpose of these conferences was to identify short-term (one to three years), medium-term (three to five years), and long-term (five to ten years) trends and challenges to Muslim regimes and to the United States. Another objective was to delineate similarities and differences in the ongoing Islamization of Muslim societies, the growing tensions between regimes and their societies, and likely regime responses to these developments. We asked academics whether the ensuing political transformation of Muslim societies would evolve gradually and peacefully or be marred by violence. The conferences and symposia usually would result in relatively short analytic reports that would be conveyed to policymakers.

From the very beginning, engaging academic experts has been designed to deepen the CIA's analytic expertise, help in-

telligence analysts sharpen their understanding of Muslim societies and discern discontinuities in those societies, and form
an ongoing partnership between government and academia for
the purpose of informing policymakers and serving the national interest and security of the United States. Over the years,
hundreds of U.S. academics with expertise in the Middle East,
Muslim countries, and Islamic activism worldwide have participated in these events, and although the conferences included mostly U.S. academics, on occasions foreign national
experts were also invited to participate. In evaluating one of the
conferences, an analyst indicated that the conference helped
him raise pertinent strategic research questions about resurgent Islamic activist movements and their long-term impact on
Muslim countries and on global relations between Muslims
and non-Muslims. On the tenth anniversary of these academic
conferences, an academic participant described the conference
as "the best U.S. government-sponsored event he has attended
in Washington in ten years." The conferences did not focus on
current American policy but on trends, options, attitudes, and
scenarios.

Apart from substantive expertise imparted by participating
professors, the academic outreach program has provided several other advantages: it encouraged analysts to seek advice
from academics on specific research projects; it instilled in analysts the value of open-source information and data, especially
the use of public opinion polls to measure Muslim attitudes toward the United States; it offered deep analysis of societal trends
and forces that drive the emergence of activists and potential
terrorists; and it summarized historical lessons that analysts
could learn from while doing current research. Academics encouraged analysts to learn from historical lessons that were pertinent to current policy, including the French occupation of
Egypt in 1798, the British experience in Iraq in the 1920s, and
Israel's experience in Lebanon in the 1980s. Participating academics contributed greatly to our analytic knowledge by discussing "lessons learned" from history. Furthermore, the meetings provided a vehicle for academics to debate the issues among
themselves and to highlight the major research questions on po-

litical Islam, which in turn informed our analysts of the ongoing research in the field. As we consulted with academics on the overarching themes of annual conferences, we always insisted that such themes be at the cutting edge of academic research. Examples included entrenched regime authoritarianism in Arab and Muslim countries; the Islamic awakening and growing Islamization; deficits in education, political reform, and women's rights in the Middle East; and civil society institutions in the Arab world.

TRAINING OF ANALYSTS

In addition to the academic outreach program, the CIA also committed resources to train its analysts and collectors in Islamic issues and languages. It hired language teachers to teach Arabic and Persian in-house, in addition to the full-time language instructors who teach in the CIA's language school, to help analysts learn a new language, maintain their proficiency level, and improve their language skills. Several years ago, my analytic unit in the Directorate of Intelligence began to offer week-long courses in Islamic studies in which a dozen academics would lecture on different topics on Islam and Muslim societies. The lectures covered themes in history, economics, leadership, theology, terminology, security, mainstream and radical ideologies, and societal transformation. These annual or semiannual courses have attracted analysts from throughout the intelligence community and have been rated highly by the participants. An analyst described the course as a "one-semester graduate course in Islamic studies crammed in one week!" A participating academic said, "I wish my advanced students could attend such a concentrated one-week course!" The agency also sent analysts to universities in the area and elsewhere for full-time academic training in Islamic studies and societies and in "Islamic" languages (Arabic, Persian, Urdu, etc.). Although the number of intelligence officers with expertise in political Islam remains arguably small and should be increased dramatically over the next five to ten years, analyst training does reflect the CIA's twofold commitment to enhance this critical expertise and to view the Muslim world beyond the prism of terrorism. The training also included sending analysts to scholarly associations' meetings and conferences and to speaking engagements at area think tanks.

The intelligence community would need to facilitate the process of hiring experts on a short-term basis, as visiting scholars or scholars in residence, to help deepen its substantive expertise in political Islam. Although academics have expressed a desire to participate in such a program, they have shied away from "taking the plunge" because of the cumbersome, intrusive, and lengthy clearance process. If the intelligence community is to succeed in hiring multicultural and multiethnic experts in "Islamic" languages, societies, and cultures, it must devise ways to simplify the security procedures in the hiring process. Of course, the more relatives an applicant has overseas and the more foreign travels he or she has made in recent years, the longer the process takes. An academic usually does not acquire recognized expertise, for example, in Arabic language and culture and in Muslim societies, without having traveled to, and done field work in, those societies and established friendships and relations with foreign nationals. This dilemma is a "catch-22" for which the intelligence community must find a solution. One possiblility might entail granting potential applicants in a relatively short order a security clearance that does not go above Confidential or Secret and might not require taking a polygraph or signing a secrecy agreement for life. These last two items have been cited by several academics as impediments to their working in the intelligence community.

CULTURAL EXPERTISE AND INTELLIGENCE ANALYSIS

Intelligence analysts have also been introduced to cultural analysis, which they are encouraged to incorporate in their products. As they are expected to provide senior policymakers with contextual analysis on Islamic issues, including the radicalization process, analysts have been strongly advised to become familiar with academic presentations and research on identity and cultural studies, a particularly useful training in the political Islam area. Analysts were taught that applying Western psychological principles, modes of knowledge, and "rational actor" models to actors and groups in non-Western, Muslim settings has limited value for intelligence work without an insider's understanding of culture and cultural discourse, language, history, society, religion, and tribal and familial linkages. They are also trained to bring several important cultural assumptions and definitions to bear on their analysis.

A culture has multiple meanings including a people's beliefs, concepts, arts, customs, language, traditions, sensitivities, emotions, and history and is part and parcel of people's living experience, how they view themselves, their relation to each other—as individuals and as a community—and their historical interaction with the "other." Islamic religious identity does not exist in a vacuum, and intelligence analysts are trained to keep in mind the contradictions and discontinuities embedded in the concept of identity and the cultural biases, empathies, and political paradigms they bring to the learning process. Analysts are introduced to such concepts as justice, honor, loyalty, friendship, hospitality, generosity, and revenge. They learn about individual and group behavior, such as personal greetings, physical gestures, blood feuds, respect for the elders and male leaders of the family or clan, and family allegiances and obligations, all of which are critical components of Arab and Muslim identity. Oftentimes, the emphasis Muslims place on some of these concepts is rarely understood in the West, and yet intelligence analysts must understand this emphasis if they are expected to produce sophisticated cultural analysis.

In Arab and Muslim societies, tribal and clan affiliations continue to influence the behavior of groups and their sense of identification; emotion is also culturally linked to Arabs' and Muslims' sense of what is morally just and religiously right, and it is an acceptable form of reaction to perceived unjust policies toward Arabs and Muslims in general. For many Arabs and Muslims, displays of strong feelings—even anger—connote deep and sincere concern about issues under discussion, but to some Westerners these displays might appear as posturing or emotional outbursts. Muslim identities today are being influ-

enced by political and social realities in Muslim countries and
the ongoing violence perpetrated against Muslims by Islamic
sectarian groups and extremists and by non-Muslims. Current
realities, as perceived by Muslims, include U.S.-led wars in Afghanistan and Iraq, a U.S.-condoned 2006 war in Lebanon,
Sunni-Shia sectarian violence in Iraq and elsewhere, Western-
supported authoritarian regimes in Arab and other Muslim
countries, a resurgent Iran, Shia revival, and continued Israeli
occupation of Palestinian and Arab lands.

In addition, Muslims believe that God revealed the scripture
to the Prophet Muhammad through the Angel Gabriel in Arabic, and the oral transmission of the faith through Arabic is an
integral part of the faith itself, which means that Arab nationalism and Islam are key underpinnings of Arab and Islamic culture. Arabic language, as embodied in the Qur'an, cuts across
both Arabism and Islam, and Arabic calligraphy has emerged as
a primary expression of Arab and Islamic art. Arabic proverbs
and metaphors, especially if they are religiously based, occupy a
central role in communication among Arabs and Muslims, who
view these metaphors as embodiment of cultural wisdom and a
sense of historical order. Finally, history lives for Arabs and
Muslims (contrast this with the Western view of history as the
"dead hand of the past"); they believe history is a living organ-
ism that continues to inform and shape the present and often
maintain an emotional attachment to their past, which frequently engenders pride, joy, anger, sadness, and sometimes an
active desire to resurrect parts of that history. Examples include
the Battle of Badr (fought by the Prophet Muhammad in 624
c.e.), the Crusades and Saladin, Qadisiyyat Saddam (the name
Saddam Husayn gave to his war with Iran in the 1980s, which
refers to a battle between the Arabs and the Persians in the seventh century), al-Nakba (a term used by Arabs to describe their
defeat by Israel in 1948 and the creation of the Jewish state), and
al-Naksa (a term used by Arabs to describe their defeat by Israel
in 1967). In most Muslim contexts, religious identity invariably
is an expression of indigenous and local agendas that do not
necessarily correspond to the global ideologies of al-Qa'ida and
other radical groups.

OPEN-SOURCE DATA MINING

Analysts were trained to incorporate information acquired from open sources into their analysis of Islamic activism. It has been a cultural thing for many analysts to think that only classified sources count in their analysis, and if a source of information is not classified (the higher classification, the better), it is not worth including. A young analyst opined, "The higher the classification, the sexier it is!" With the explosion of the Internet, with its databases, Web sites, and blogs, available data on Islamic activism in different languages have become mind-boggling. Analysts have been encouraged to explore blogs, Web sites, Google searches, foreign satellite television interviews, foreign-language publications, writings of academics and other private-sector experts, academic conferences, think tanks publications, the media, and foreign organizations and NGOs. Frequently, these databases and Web sites offer rich data and a wealth of information that classified reporting cannot match. The problem of highly classified analysis is that it reaches a very small number of policymakers. In order to change the culture of analysis, the intelligence community has embarked on training analysts on the efficacy of open-source materials and the necessity to use such materials in their analysis. Information obtained from these sources does not replace secretly obtained data, but it does complement it very strongly. Analysts are being trained to develop open-source intelligence (OSINT) and incorporate data obtained from it in their analysis as a matter of course. They are also encouraged to explore and develop sophisticated techniques to mine unclassified sources, and in 2005 the director of national intelligence established a freestanding Open Source Center to showcase the value of intelligence obtained from unclassified sources and to help analysts adopt a new mind-set about their value. Analysts have been urged to delve into different Islamic Web sites, both Sunni and Shia, and analyze the diverse ideological trends among Muslim activists, the factors underpinning Sunni-Shia sectarianism, and the theological debates among Muslim thinkers and in newspaper editorials—most of which are not translated into English.

In addition, intelligence analysts are being trained in advanced analytic techniques to help them do trends, opportunity, and scenario analysis; avoid the trap of "mind-sets" grounded in expertise; and be willing to reexamine their assumptions about a certain country, group, leader, or movement if the signposts have changes or new information becomes available. In fact, classified information obtained surreptitiously is only a very small portion of all available information on any one topic. Contextual data—economic, demographic, historical, political, and social—are invariably obtained from open sources and rarely from classified sources. Furthermore, closed, denied, or hard-target countries are by definition difficult to penetrate, which means that analysts must rely on information obtained from the public domain or from third-country nationals for their analysis. In these situations, there is much opportunity to "steal" information; in other cases, information is not worth "stealing." Open-source information is rapidly becoming indispensable for intelligence analysis, requiring analysts to allot more time in their daily schedule to mine data through the Internet and other electronic venues.

VISITING MUSLIM COUNTRIES

In an effort to expand analysts' knowledge of the Muslim world and provide them an opportunity to understand the diversity and complexity of different Muslim societies and cultures, the CIA in the past decade and a half has provided resources for analysts to visit numerous countries and engage interlocutors across the Muslim world. This support provided me the opportunity to visit dozens of Muslim countries over the years and allowed me to produce valuable reports informed by personal interviews and on-site investigations. However, these visits were fraught with challenges. Some analysts quickly discovered that to engage Muslim activists and thinkers in serious discussions, they have to be knowledgeable of the issues and fluent in local languages. A senior agency person in the field said, "Your interlocutors would dismiss your questions if they concluded that you didn't know what the hell you were talking about. Muslim contacts tend to speak freely when they are talking in their own language, especially in Arabic, but once they see an interpreter in the room, they clam up!" I experienced this situation on a visit I made to a Central Asian country. A week before I got there, a local young cleric spoke to a visiting CIA director about the conditions in that country through an interpreter. He basically gave the director the government line. When I met the young cleric a few days later and spoke to him in Arabic, he opened up and told me a different story of the government's view toward political Islam and offered useful information about mosques closed by the regime and clerics arrested or "made to disappear" by the security services. This incident highlighted two points: Muslim activists do not trust interpreters and view them as agents of the regime, and non-Arabic Muslims feel proud to converse in Arabic because it reflects a "noble" effort on their part to study the divine language of the Qur'an. Visits to dozens of Muslim countries and interaction with hundreds of Islamic activists have given me and other intelligence analysts the opportunity "to experience the smells and sounds of Muslim societies and feel what's going on in local neighborhoods and in the *suq* [marketplace]." The more senior and experienced the analyst, the more productive the trip usually is because of the depth of interviews the analyst can conduct with Muslim political leaders, political party activists, and civil society representatives. At the conclusion of these trips, a report is often prepared to brief senior policymakers on specific countries and groups; a summary of the trip report is sometimes included in the President's Daily Brief or PDB.

Unfortunately, the intelligence community has a very small number of senior analysts with language and cultural expertise in political Islam and Muslim societies in general. A relatively high percentage of the analytic work force consists of junior analysts with fewer than three years' experience and limited proficiency in Arabic, Persian, or Urdu. Even after an analyst goes through a year of full-time language training in Arabic or Persian, the test score at the end of the year is nowhere equivalent to native proficiency. A middle-of-the-scale score allows the analyst to carry on social conversation and read newspaper headlines but not to engage in nuanced discussion about politics, theology, leadership motivations, economic policies, or social mobilization. Because even two years of full-time Arabic-language training is insufficient, the Department of State decided to expand its Arabic-language program at its language school to three years. The intelligence community would benefit significantly from expanding its language program now that its analytic work force is growing.

ANALYTIC PRODUCTS, BRIEFINGS, AND POLICYMAKERS' RESPONSE

As the CIA systematically began building its expertise in political Islam in the early 1990s, it started producing current and long-term strategic analytic reports on the issue. Some of these products also included baseline analysis of Islamic activism, which in the early 1990s was described by Islamic activists in Saudi Arabia and elsewhere as the "Islamic Awakening" or *al-sahwa al-Islamiyya*. The CIA was the first U.S. government agency to produce a major product, sort of a primer, on global Islamic trends and ideologies, which was widely disseminated throughout the intelligence and policy communities. The analytic arm of the agency also produced strategic analyses on Islamic economics, leadership, education and school curricula, media, political parties, and movements (such as the Muslim Brotherhood), as well as on moderate and radical Muslim thinkers and opinion makers. These products, which comprised short and long research papers, National Intelligence Estimates, TDY trip reports, conference reports, short memoranda, and PDB articles, often became the focus of high-level briefings that CIA senior analysts gave to policymakers in the executive branch and in Congress, especially the intelligence committees. These briefings, grounded in the rapidly expanding knowledge of political Islam within the CIA, began to generate growing interest within the policy community on this issue. Initially, the analytic products and briefings focused on political Islam in the Middle East, but since 2001 they began to encompass Islamic activism worldwide.

Despite the fact that CIA briefings had no political ax to grind and were not policy prescriptive, senior policymakers who were committed to toppling Saddam Husayn and who pushed a specific policy posture in the Middle East frequently ignored the worst-case scenario that could ensue following a war in Iraq. Some White House, National Security Council, and Department of Defense senior officials went so far as to accuse the CIA of being opposed to the Bush administration, or simply not being "on the same sheet of music." Certain CIA analytic pieces were viewed as too alarmist or too critical of administration policy. Policymakers often used CIA expert analysts as a research resource and listened to analysts' briefings and analysis, which they viewed as one of many voices that impacted policy. The briefings included data we collected from the field through clandestine and open-source methods, numerous interviews we conducted with Islamic activists, and classified reports we received from our own government and other friendly governments and intelligence services worldwide. The analyses focused on what Iraq could look like after the American invasion, how American-style democracy could be implemented in Arab and Muslim countries, which Muslims should or should not be allowed to participate in the political process, and how the United States could deal with the so-called moderate regimes that were authoritarian and corrupt but friendly to the United States. Although our analysts knew that the CIA did not make policy, that ours was one of many voices policymakers listened to, analysts were often frustrated because they assessed that certain policies did not resonate well in the Arab Muslim world and did not serve America's long-term national security and interests.

IRAQ: CRITICAL BRIEFINGS BEFORE AND AFTER THE INVASION

Many books and journal articles have been written on the Iraq war since it started in the spring of 2003 and the Bush administration's rationale for invading Iraq and removing Saddam

Husayn and his regime. Much media analysis, pro- and antiadministration, has been offered about whether the administration's action was the result of flawed intelligence before the war or whether the war was a foregone conclusion regardless of the intelligence. The analysis in this chapter, however, does not review previous arguments or assess policy but focuses on the critical briefings the agency presented to the administration on the eve of and during the war regarding the Iraqi state, the Iraqi people's reaction to the occupation, the nature of the insurgency, the role of the Shia leadership, and the regional implications of the American occupation of the "heart of Islam."

Unfortunately, many of the "inside the Beltway" books and official reports that have appeared since the start of the war have focused on such issues as whether the White House was provided with accurate intelligence, or the meaning of former CIA director George Tenet's "slam dunk" statement, or the tensions between the administration and the CIA. Much of this analysis misses the point. The core issue of the war, I think, is threefold: first, the administration decided to go to war right after 9/11 regardless of what intelligence it had or the quality of that intelligence; second, war advocates within the administration misunderstood the nature of Iraqi society and the long-term implications of an American-led war of choice on the region; and, third, they did not pay attention to the nuanced analysis of the intelligence community on the complexity of Iraq's Arab, Sunni, and Shia regional context. Our briefings informed the administration that defeating Saddam's army and toppling his regime were not the real challenge to the United States; planning for the "morning after" was the true challenge. It was critical for the administration to have a clear idea of what impact the occupation would have on Iraqi society and not to confuse Iraqis' hatred for Saddam with their love for the occupation. In his book, *At the Center of the Storm* (2007, 307), Tenet relates an incident that I experienced at a meeting with a senior NSC official right after 9/11. When the official told me that the administration was determined to get rid of Saddam, I said, "If you want to go after that son of a bitch to settle old scores, be my guest. But don't tell us he is connected to 9/11 or to terrorism because there is no evidence to support that. You will have to have a better reason."

While Iraqis would welcome American military action to remove Saddam, they would not want us to stay as occupiers; the so-called liberation would very quickly turn into occupation. Bringing Iraqi exiles from the outside to run the country would not be welcomed by Iraqis who suffered under Saddam's brutal rule while these exiles enjoyed the luxury of living in the West. "The Ritz nomads [moving from one Ritz-Carlton to another] have lost touch with the realities of Iraq," said an Iraqi academic describing the life of Iraqi exiles. Playing the sectarian card, especially promoting one sect over another, and marginalizing the Sunnis would be disastrous for the future of Iraq. Nation building in Iraq and reordering Iraqi society in the image of Pentagon war planners without a deep knowledge of Iraqi society and culture and of the surrounding Arab-Islamic environment had only a minimal chance of success. Neighboring Sunni states would not look with favor upon a Shia Iraq as a shining beacon of democracy and pluralism to emulate. Furthermore, academic scholars of Iraq generally agreed that dissolving the army and de-Ba'thification would not be welcomed by the Iraqi people and would instantly create a huge pool of unemployed, disgruntled Iraqis who would turn against the occupation.

Academic research and newspaper articles from the region indicated that viewing Iraq in a vacuum isolated from its regional context would create untold challenges for the United States and would make neighboring states hesitant to get involved in the occupation efforts. A lengthy occupation of Baghdad, the symbol of Islam's "golden age," would be perceived by Muslims as another anti-Islamic and anti-Arab policy by the United States. Playing the Shia card, as Israel did in Lebanon in the 1980s, might net short-term benefits, but in the long run it would not produce positive results for the occupation. While Iraqi Shia, especially Grand Ayatollah Ali al-Husayni Sistani, supported the removal of Saddam Husayn and endorsed the concepts of national elections and a secular pluralist Iraq, their sole purpose was to come to power, defeat the Sunnis, and settle old scores.

According to academic scholars on Shia Islam, Sistani's persistent support for elections was mistakenly interpreted in Washington as acquiescence in the continued occupation of Iraq. Nor were Iraqi Shia as monolithic as some senior policymakers believed. Different trends existed within Iraqi Shia, ranging from Sistani's quietist camp to Muqtada al-Sadr's more activist and confrontational attitude toward the American-led occupation. Academic studies at the time urged policymakers to pay special attention to the complex relations Iraqi Shia leaders had with Iran, where a number of them had resided during much of the past thirty years. Shia leaders' innate desire to reconcile their Iraqi Arab identity with their religious, political, and historical ties to Iran was not fully appreciated by senior policymakers as they were trying to manage post-Saddam Iraq. For example, they did not show much interest in the rising tensions between the Iraqi Shia ayatollahs at Najaf and Karbala and their Iranian counterparts in Qom, or the influence that Iraqi senior clerics enjoyed throughout the region and the relationships they had forged over the years with regional religious leaders such as Shaykh Muhammad Hussein Fadlallah, the spiritual leader of Hizballah and Lebanese Shia.

We prepared detailed briefings on the subject covering the role of Najaf and Karbala in Shia history and theology, the relation between the Shia theological centers or *hawzas* in these two places and those in Qom in Iran, the different centers of theological influence among Iraqi Shia, the rise of the populist cleric Muqtada al-Sadr, and the history of Shia-Sunni relations in Iraq and in neighboring states. The briefings did not propose specific policies but analyzed the potential impact of specific policies the administration might adopt toward the Shia on sectarian politics in Iraq and on regional states, especially Jordan, Iran, and Saudi Arabia. Arab Sunni leaders in the region began to warn against the rise of what they called a "Shia Crescent" in the greater Middle East from Lebanon to Pakistan. American policymakers did not meet face-to-face with Sistani and relied instead on conduits to explain his positions on issues critical to the political restructuring of Iraq.

For many months, the leadership at the Pentagon and at the

White House failed to acknowledge the existence of the insurgency and even banned the use of the word "insurgency" from official briefings, arguing that the opposition to U.S. forces came from "Ba'thists, remnants of the Saddam regime, disgruntled Sunnis, criminals, and pro– al-Qaʿida terrorists." Once administration officials finally accepted the assessment that an insurgency indeed was afoot in Iraq, they attributed it to foreign fighters and al-Qaʿida. According to media reports, the realities in Iraq included widespread support of the insurgency among Iraqi Sunnis, antioccupation nationalists, pro-Sadr Shia, al-Qaʿida in Iraq, the Zarqawi group, and foreign fighters or jihadists. As the administration began to raise the specter of foreign jihadists in Iraq in earnest as the central component of the insurgency, media reports from the region indicated that the numbers of foreign fighters did not exceed several thousand at most and that the insurgency comprised many more opponents to the occupation than that. Iraq as a breeding ground for terrorists and jihadists became a self-fulfilling prophecy. Before the war there was no evidence of high-level ties between Saddam Husayn and Usama Bin Ladin, but after the United States invaded Iraq, al-Qaʿida began to use Iraq as a recruiting ground for global jihad. Unfortunately, the mismanagement of Iraq after the spring of 2003 provided al-Qaʿida with a ready-made environment for its operations. The link between Iraq and al-Qaʿida, which President Bush has often cited as a justification for the continued occupation of that country, emerged after the invasion of Iraq, not before it.

The other Iraq-centric issue we briefed the administration after 2003 was the rising Sunni-Shia sectarian violence and its long-term impact on Iraqi society and on the region. Thousands of Iraqis, Sunni and Shia, were forced to move from their homes to other neighborhoods because of sectarian affiliation; thousands others have been killed for the same reason. The entire so-called democratic process in post-Saddam Iraq—elections, political parties and slates, allotment of parliamentary seats and government positions, distribution of resources, employment opportunities, and patronage—is grounded in sectarian politics, and while the administration spoke of a liberal, democratic, pluralistic Iraq, sectarianism was becoming deeply entrenched in that society. Neighboring Sunni states and religious leaders began to denounce the sectarian violence against Iraqi Sunnis, indicating that they would come to the aid of the Sunni community—militarily, economically, and politically. Arab Sunni leaders in neighboring countries feared the long-term impact of sectarianism on the region and expressed concerns that, if sectarian violence in Iraq goes unchecked, it would spread to other countries in the region. The deepening quagmire in Iraq in the past five years has made sectarianism a fundamental challenge to stability in the Middle East and South Asia. Consequently, Sunni-Shia relations across the region have become more tense and fragile, and Sunni 'ulama, especially in Saudi Arabia, have engaged in vitriol against Shia Muslims, accusing them of apostasy and infidelity. Because of the Iraqi experience, it will take years for Sunni and Shia Muslims to reconcile their differences and overcome their suspicions. The political system that was created in post-Saddam Iraq was inherently sectarian favoring the Shia, a system that understandably was promoted and defended by the Iraqi Shia leadership to serve the interests of the Shia community. It is imperative that scholars analyze the long-term strategic challenges that such a system would have for the United States in its relations with Sunni Muslim states in the region and beyond.

In his book *At the Center of the Storm,* former CIA director Tenet attributes the failure to address the challenges facing the United States after the invasion to failed American policy in post-Saddam Iraq. War advocates within the administration were determined to go after Saddam and believed they could use American power to create a new Middle East and restructure Arab society from within, regardless of the realities on the ground. They often accused anyone who would raise a cautionary flag about the invasion as soft on terrorism or not fully on board with the administration's global vision. That was what underpinned the Pentagon's attacks on the CIA and the creation of a parallel intelligence gathering and analysis group outside existing intelligence community agencies. The arguments about Saddam's weapons programs or the quality of intelligence that were voiced by senior policymakers as a justification of the war or of what went wrong in Iraq after 2003 were extremely marginal in the decision to invade Iraq. Administration war planners probably understood early on that their ideological vision of the "new" Middle East did not match Iraqi and regional realities but proceeded with their war plans regardless. According to press reports, not one of the half dozen most senior policymakers involved in the war had a deep expertise in the Middle East or in Arab or Islamic culture and society, but this lack of expertise did not prevent them from invading and occupying a major Arab country. Press reports began to question administration officials about what would happen after U.S. troops withdraw from Iraq. Administration spokesmen, from the president down, have constantly claimed that if the U.S. withdraws anytime soon, the country "would fall apart." However, most regional experts were in agreement that Iraqis, not foreigners, will ultimately decide whether Iraq would remain a unified country and whether the different Iraqi factions would opt for national reconciliation or continue on the path of violence.

As Iraqi national, ethnic, and tribal loyalties have transformed dramatically since the invasion, these loyalties, not a foreigner's imagined view of them, will determine the future of Iraq. Staying or withdrawing will not make much of a difference. Iraqi leaders who inhabit the "Green Zone" are equally clueless about what is happening in the country and are perhaps the only Iraqis who have any faith left in the usefulness of the continued occupation because of the personal and financial benefits they derive from it. The administration's dire predictions about the future of Iraq in the wake of a precipitous withdrawal might resonate well with segments of the American public and the Washington, D.C., media but not with Iraqis who view it as patronizing and divorced from reality. Even Iraqis who work closely with the occupation as translators and guides and who live with U.S. Army units have also come to resent the condescending and discriminatory treatment they experience in these units. According to some media reports, Iraqis eat separately, use different toilets, and often are forced to enter through different doors. This treatment is not done for security reasons because Iraqis who work in these units have been vetted and have the requisite security clearances.

MUSLIM BROTHERHOOD, HAMAS, AND THE AMERICAN RESPONSE

Intelligence community briefings on political Islam covered the role of Islamic parties in political reform and democratization and ways to engage them in the political process. The Muslim Brotherhood (MB) has not been allowed to run candidates in Egyptian elections under its name but only as "independents." Hamas ran in Palestinian elections and won an impressive victory. Most scholars of the region agree that genuine political transformation and even democratization in Muslim societies could not occur without involving mainstream Islamic political parties in the process. These parties in several Muslim countries have been involved in national politics for many years. In non-Arab states, from Turkey to Indonesia, Islamic parties have participated in national elections for years without much opposition from the United States. In the Arab states, however, two developments occurred: Islamic political parties were opposed by pro-U.S. autocratic regimes and therefore were not allowed to participate fully in the process; and Hamas, a terrorist group under U.S. law, won the elections in Palestine. In the first instance, when pro-U.S. regimes denied Islamic political parties the right to participate in national elections, the United States did not object, arguing that the issue was "an internal matter." Direct contacts between the U.S. Embassy and the MB were halted in the late 1990s because of objections from the regime of Hosni Mubarak.

Arab and Islamic media reports, pro-MB newspaper and electronic articles (www.ikhwanonline.com), interviews with MB activists, and academic analysis have indicated that the MB would respond favorably to contacts by American officials, that the MB leadership was seriously interested in participating in the political system in Egypt despite its historic opposition to the Mubarak regime, and that it was committed to the long-term stability of Egypt. The U.S. government has yet to approve contacts with the MB; however, a senior State Department official allowed that U.S. Embassy officers in Cairo could talk to the elected members of the MB as elected members of parliament ("because we talk to all parliamentarians," according to a State Department spokesman), but not as members of the Muslim Brotherhood. The deeply ingrained Muslim culture of Egypt makes it almost impossible to pursue political reform in that country without the involvement of the Muslim Brotherhood and its supporters. Academic experts on Egypt have argued that, because of regime opposition to a meaningful reform, a genuine transformation of society will be driven ultimately by forces from below. MB sympathies cut across the different segments of Egyptian society, from the highly professional class to the barely educated youth, and many professional associations have elected MB members to lead them. According to Egyptian opposition media reports and academic analysis, the Mubarak regime has contended that allowing the MB to enter the political process would create chaos similar to what has happened in Iraq, Palestine, and Lebanon. The worn-out argument of equating autocracy with stability might be useful in the short term, but it will undermine America's long-term interests in the region, especially as the United States continues to proclaim its support for democracy and aversion to tyranny.

In the case of Hamas, regional observers and experts agreed that American objections to the election results were much more crippling to the new government, resulting in increased poverty among Palestinians and in freezing all possibilities for negotiations between Israel and the Palestinians, which the Bush administration had initially sponsored. The Bush administration decided to boycott the Hamas government and suspend all aid to government institutions, creating a bad situation for the Palestinian people. The CIA, especially its former director George Tenet, had deep expertise in the Palestinian-Israeli issue and provided thoughtful analysis and briefings on the subject. Director Tenet established and nurtured strong relations with regional leaders on the Palestinian question and gained their respect for his interest, expertise, and commitment. As a

CIA colleague quipped, "George Tenet was really a DCI for the Middle East!"

Hamas's impressive electoral victory, which no one had expected, generated a completely negative reaction in Washington despite the fact that the United States had pushed hard for Palestinian elections. Many moderate Arab and Muslim thinkers argued following the elections that a U.S. boycott of Hamas would send the wrong signal to the Arab Muslim world and would indicate in effect that America supports democracy only conditionally and endorses elections only when they promise favorable results in advance. Such a position would also signal to the Muslim world that Islamic political parties are not really welcome in the political process. According to these thinkers, the Hamas victory reflected Palestinian disgust with the corrupt, sleazy, and incompetent politics of Fatah and the Palestinian Authority. The vote for Hamas did not indicate a shift among Palestinians toward more religiosity or Islamic radicalism, nor was it a part of a global process of radicalization. In fact, al-Qaʿida's leadership strongly criticized Hamas for participating in the elections. The Palestinian electorate voted for Hamas because of its nationalist credentials, service to the community, and reputation for honesty and because the Palestinian Authority had lost its credibility and legitimacy long before the elections. Academic experts argued at the time that, by boycotting Hamas and working actively to undermine the Hamas-led government, the United States and other Western governments squandered an opportunity to push the Israeli-Palestinian peace process forward, and the promised two-state solution in Palestine has all but disappeared.

We made several important points in our briefings to senior policymakers on the role of mainstream Islamic political parties in the process of political reform and democratization in their societies. First, many mainstream Islamic political parties in the past ten years have emerged across the Muslim world as genuine agents of democratization and credible advocates of political reform; in the past few years, these parties seemed to have shifted from being antiregime dissidents on the margins of politics to serious players at the heart of the democratization process. Second, despite potential tensions between Islamic parties' adherence to *Sharia* and their democratic practices, the metric by which we measure the commitment of these parties to "man-made" democracy—predicated on inclusiveness, pluralism, compromise, and minority and women's rights—should be based on their performance and political pragmatism, not their religious ideology. Third, most Islamic political parties and groups—including the Muslim Brotherhood in Egypt, Jordan, and Syria; Hamas in Palestine; Hizballah in Lebanon; the Islamic Party of Malaysia; al-Nahda in Tunisia; Justice and Charity in Morocco; the Islamic Party in Kenya; the AKP in Turkey; and the Prosperous Justice Party in Indonesia—appear to be committed to the concept and practice of democracy and have participated, or desire to participate, in national elections. Many of these Muslim parliamentarians have in fact become adept at political compromise in order to pass specific pieces of legislation and have become comfortable with the whole process of legislative politics.

By voting for these parties, the electorate expects them to offer a fresh and exciting vision of the future and a credible substitute to the discredited secular nationalist paradigm associated in the minds of the electorate with poor governance and failed regimes. The electorates in many Muslim countries are becoming more sophisticated and discriminating and generally do not vote for radical parties and their candidates. Islamic political parties that tend to overemphasize their Islamic credentials have not done well in national elections; their electoral campaigns and agendas have reflected a sophisticated sense of pragmatism and awareness of the realities of their societies.

AUTHORITARIAN REGIMES AND POLITICAL REFORM

According to academic analysis, pro-U.S. authoritarian regimes in the Middle East region have used their close relations with the United States, especially after 9/11, as well as the chaos in Iraq to thwart America's strategic support for democracy and political reform in those countries. They have often relied on

Washington's perceived need of their support in counterterrorism as a crutch to suppress any opposition to their rule and all demands for political reform and have led their people to believe that United States' close relationship with them indicated American support for their governance. Liberal, secular elites have been harassed by these regimes and are often arrested and jailed without much American opposition. As one Egyptian secularist told me, "Now that Washington has ignored Islamic political parties and turned a blind eye to the poor human rights policies of these regimes, how do you Americans expect to bring democracy to our region?" Academic experts have argued that the diminishing legitimacy of authoritarian Arab regimes—the result of corruption, nepotism, repression, and violations of human rights—has led them to use the rhetoric of democracy to cement their hold on power; at the same time, moderate groups in several countries that were ready to engage the United States on issues of political reform and challenge radical Islamic activists now feel isolated and marginalized. In many Arab countries, there is little room for them in the public space that is dominated by regimes and, to a lesser extent, by the radical paradigm.

The intelligence briefings raised questions about how long these regimes could continue to count on American support in their use of the terrorism card to defend their undemocratic policies. More and more reports were coming out of the region indicating that pro-democracy reformers were losing effectiveness and credibility and unable to pursue a reformist agenda because of the absence of outside support, especially from the United States. A Jordanian reformist thinker said, "These regimes are smart and know how to speak the language that resonates well in Washington. In the old days, they used the anticommunist language; today, they use the antiterrorism language, and Uncle Sam always comes to the rescue!" Our analysts frequently heard similar statements on visits to these countries. TDY briefings on what they heard were frequently given to senior policymakers at the State Department and the NSC, especially to officials directly involved in the American democracy initiative. Almost always, big policy issues, such as Iraq, terrorism, the Arab-Israeli question, Iran, and Afghanistan trumped the democracy initiative despite the personal interest of a few senior policymakers, and regimes often were able to convince senior American officials that domestic stability, not democracy, was the overriding regional issue. A Saudi reformer told me, "Regimes have convinced the United States since 9/11 and especially since the Iraq invasion that domestic security—meaning their survival—was existential and democracy was only a luxury, and of course it was a no brainer which one of the two would take precedence!" CIA director Tenet has advocated the need to reach out to reformist forces in Arab countries, and President Bush has given eloquent speeches in defense of democracy, but authoritarian regime stability continues to trump democracy.

BUREAUCRATIC IMPEDIMENTS

In building expertise in political Islam, the CIA, like the rest of the U.S. government, has not been immune to bureaucratic delays, infighting, and rivalries. Two examples are illustrative. The first involves institutionalizing the agency's analytic expertise on political Islam, and the second deals with expanding the collection of data on Islamic activism. The information, collected from all kinds of sources, is the bread and butter of analysis.

Early in this decade, a proposal was submitted to establish a senior-level analytic unit in the Directorate of Intelligence to examine the Muslim world systematically and to do sophisticated, in-depth analysis of the growing Islamization of Muslim societies, the rising involvement of Muslim political parties in the political process, the ideological debate among Muslim thinkers on the future of their religion, and the expanding role of formal and informal Islamic NGOs in spreading the faith among Muslims and non-Muslims and in cementing linkages among Muslim activists worldwide. The proposed unit was to operate on the assumption that Islam as a religion was not the enemy of the United States and that the American government did not intend to target Muslims or their religion. A related assumption was that the Muslim world is much larger than the minority of terrorists and that the U.S. government must dedicate resources to understanding a religion to which 1.4 billion people adhere. To do that requires attention to the economics, education, demography, government, history, ideology, language and literature, leadership, politics, political parties and party activists, religion, and social forces in Muslim societies. Another part of the central thesis of the proposal was that enhanced expertise in these areas not only contributed to the expanding of analysts' knowledge but was also critical to American national security. Simply put, in order to design and implement effective and rational policies toward the Islamic world and the fight against terrorism and terrorists, the U.S. government must first understand the context and environment that give rise to extremism and terrorism, the concerns that occupy Muslims worldwide, Muslims' vision of Islam's role in the world, and actions—lawful and unlawful—that some Islamic activists take toward each other and toward non-Muslims based on their interpretation of their faith.

The proposal was favorably received from day one and was implemented in 2004, two years after it was submitted. CIA leadership welcomed the proposal and supported the creation of a separate entity, which included analysts, support staff, supplies, and office space. It voiced support of the concept, was enthused about the need to undertake a new initiative, and promised to move quickly. Despite budgetary constraints and understandable bureaucratic "stove piping" impediments, the agency leadership saw the urgent need for such a program, especially when one considers that the country was facing a growing global challenge about which we knew very little.

Senior managers supported the idea of deepening the agency's expertise in political Islam. Although the memory of the terrorist attacks of 2001 was still vivid in people's minds, the U.S. government was woefully unprepared to deal with the Islamic world because of limited expertise in the subject. Agency managers conceded that political Islam was a global phenomenon stretching from Marrakech to Bangladesh and from Istanbul to Jakarta, which must be systematically studied and analyzed. The new unit became the center of expertise throughout the government on political Islam issues, and despite its relatively small staff, the unit produced significant publications and reports that were well received by senior "customers" downtown. When we briefed the new unit to senior policymakers at the NSC and members of the intelligence committees in Congress, the reaction was uniformly positive and curious as to why it took the CIA three years after 9/11 to establish such a unit. After one of those briefings, the then deputy national security advisor asked, "How come you waited so long?"

Although members of the congressional intelligence committees' senior staff welcomed the creation of the political Islam unit, they urged that more resources be diverted to it because of the strategic importance of its mission and the need to expand the government's expertise in Islam. One senior staffer told me that, "although Islamic terrorists are a tiny minority, we as a government need to understand why they are Islamic terrorists, why they use Islam as a justification for their terrorism, and how were they allowed by other Muslims to hijack their religion and put it on a collision course with the West." Policymakers could benefit immensely from the CIA's expertise in various aspects of political Islam in forging public diplomacy toward the Islamic world and assessing how different segments in Muslim societies would respond to policy initiatives. Although the creation of the political Islam unit reflected the agency's commitment to enhancing its expertise on the topic, it is imperative that the analytic cadre in the unit be expanded over time and the senior leadership's commitment to this unit be maintained.

COLLECTING DATA ON POLITICAL ISLAM

Enhancing government expertise in political Islam requires that collection on this topic be expanded and systematized. As the intelligence community collects information on issues that are critical to U.S. national interests and security, it is imperative that "political Islam" be included. According to the director of national intelligence, the six basic intelligence collection sources include signals intelligence or SIGINT (derived from signal intercepts, under the responsibility of the National Security

Agency), imagery intelligence or IMINT (representations of objects reproduced electronically or through photography or radar sensors, managed by the National Geospatial Agency), measurement and signals intelligence or MASINT (technically derived intelligence other than imagery and SIGINT, managed by an entity in the Defense Intelligence Agency), human intelligence or HUMINT (derived from human sources and used primarily by the CIA, the Department of State, the Department of Defense, and the FBI and managed by the director of the CIA), and open-source intelligence or OSINT (publicly available information appearing in print or electronic media, managed by the Open Source Center under the office of the director of national intelligence). CIA analysts rely heavily on human collection; however, in order to get the information from the field, they usually send requests or "requirements" asking for specific information on leaders, groups, movements, organizations, thinkers, activists, political parties, and economic, educational, and demographic data, as well as other kinds of information that might give collectors and analysts, and ultimately policymakers, a clear idea of the motivations and capabilities of other countries and groups. Collectors collect data on topics that are usually included in a government-approved list of national priority topics. When an analyst sends a request to a particular embassy requesting certain information, the collector reviews the list to make sure the issue is on it. If not, the request gets a low priority and is addressed if time and resources are available.

After the establishment of the political Islam unit, it was suggested that data on the issue should be collected separately, because after 9/11 Islamic activism clearly became a critical issue for the United States. In fact, many Muslim thinkers urged the American government after 9/11 to take a more comprehensive view of the Islamic world and not to stick the terrorism label on all Muslims. Hundreds of Muslim thinkers and scholars condemned the terrorist attacks of 9/11 and accused al-Qaʻida and Bin Ladin of misinterpreting and misrepresenting Islam. Because of these views, it became imperative for the U.S. government to collect more data on political Islam and acquire a more sophisticated knowledge on the topic, which comes through collection and analysis.

Proponents of a separate collection strategy on political Islam further argued that other terms in social, political, and radical activism do not adequately cover the issue because political Islam is much wider than terrorism and because political instability is irrelevant in stable democracies where Islamic activism is on the rise. Terrorism and political instability might apply to Saudi Arabia or Pakistan, for example, but not to France or Holland. It is not clear as of this writing whether the "Principals' Meeting," or "PC" as it is known in Washington, which comprises the most senior leaders of the administration, cabinet secretaries, the director of central intelligence, and the chairman of the Joint Chiefs of Staff or their representatives, has discussed the issue. I cite this case to show how bureaucratic delays can be so detrimental to our national security at a time when Islamic activism has grown by leaps and bounds among Muslim communities worldwide. When I asked an Arabic-speaking senior officer at an American embassy in the Middle East about political Islam, he said, "Of course, I understand the criticality of this issue, but if I am not required to deal with it, I'll get to it *inshallah bukra* (God willing tomorrow) when I have sufficient resources, which I don't."

Chapter 3

PUBLIC DIPLOMACY: ISSUES AND ATTITUDES

MANY PUBLIC OPINION POLLS and press reports have indicated that American public diplomacy in the Muslim world since September 11, 2001, has failed to reach out to Muslims and convince them that the so-called global war on terror is not a war against Islam. According to a variety of public opinion polls (Pew, Gallup, State Department, BBC, University of Maryland, Zogby, etc.), American standing, prestige, likeability, and trust in the past half decade have been rated very low, and although these high unfavorability ratings vary among Muslim countries, the overall trend has been negative throughout the Muslim world. Furthermore, the United States has been viewed in some of these polls as a threat to world peace, an arrogant superpower engaged in military conflicts against Islam and the Arab world, and not interested in the promotion of democracy and economic welfare for Muslim peoples. Conversations with hundreds of interlocutors—secular and practicing Muslims—persuaded me that their negative views of the United States are driven by policies, not ideas or values, and that these views are not limited to radicals or jihadists but cut across different segments of society, including highly educated and pro-Western liberal professionals. Winning the battle of the hearts and minds of millions of Muslims requires that the U.S. government adopt creative, sophisticated, and forward-looking strategies that address different audiences in different countries through tangible programs and initiatives.

The old ways of parsing official speeches to appease different audiences no longer work. Muslim publics are becoming more educated and nuanced; many of them speak and read English and follow American political news and statements closely. The so-called Arab street or Islamic street—implying some sort of a mob mentality—has been replaced by well-informed and technologically connected publics; villages and hamlets in the Fergana Valley in Central Asia, for example, are no longer isolated settlements but are wired to a globalized world. In reference to this point, a Muslim interlocutor commented, "We might be poor and we might be weak, but we are not stupid; we know what's going on around us!" Negative trends are reversible, and if the United States sees that it is in the national interest to implement different policies, it would be possible to regain its reputation for honesty, fairness, and justice among Muslim publics. Of course, American policy cannot possibly address the entire gamut of Muslim grievances—many of which have nothing to do with the United States—but it is possible to find common ground for a cooperative and mutually beneficial relationship.

The attitudes gathered through anecdotes and statements collected from numerous interviews are corroborated in recent public opinion surveys conducted by the Gallup Organization in 2006 in ten predominantly Muslim countries, by the World Public Opinion project at the University of Maryland in December 2005–January 2006 in four Muslim countries, and by the Pew Global Attitudes Project in 2004 and 2005 in seventeen Muslim and non-Muslim countries. In the Gallup poll, when the interviewees were asked to agree or disagree with the statement that the United States was serious about the establishment of democratic systems in Muslims regions, almost two-thirds of respondents in Jordan, Egypt, and Morocco and more than half in Iran, Pakistan, Turkey, Lebanon, and Indonesia indicated they disagreed with the statement. When asked to agree or disagree with the statement that the United States was serious about improving the economic lot of the people in their region, more than two-thirds in Jordan, Egypt, Iran, Pakistan, Turkey, Morocco, and Lebanon and more than half in Indonesia disagreed with the statement. According to Gallup, the low favorability ratings of the United States in Muslim countries between 2001 and 2005 almost remained the same. However, the unfavorability ratings in Turkey and Saudi Arabia have increased significantly—31 percentage points in Turkey and 15 points in Saudi Arabia. When asked whether their constitution should include freedoms of speech, religion, and assembly, overwhelming majorities in the ten countries agreed with the statement, indicating that their negative views of the United States are not driven by American values but by specific policies perceived by them as anti-Arab or anti-Islamic.

The results also indicate that the divide between Muslims and the Christian West that has been touted by Bin Ladin and other radicals does not reflect the attitudes of Muslim majorities, nor do these majorities see the world with the same dark lenses as al-Qa'ida does. Many highly educated and economically prosperous Muslims see no contradiction between their criticism of American foreign policy and their desire to visit the United States, buy American products, benefit from American technology, study in American universities, and engage American diplomats. A few year ago when I asked a Muslim young man, who was standing in line near a U.S. consulate seeking a visa, why he wanted to go to America, he replied, "you have good education, you have freedom, and I hear Muslims do well in your country." That same person would without hesitation criticize American "anti-Islamic" foreign policy. The attitudes expressed in this and many other anecdotes are captured in the polls.

POLLS AND ATTITUDES

The University of Maryland–supported World Public Opinion (WorldPublicOpinion.org) issued a report on an in-depth survey of public opinion on American policy that it conducted in Egypt, Indonesia, Morocco, and Pakistan between December 2006 and February 2007. This comprehensive survey offered several important findings about how majorities of Muslims in the four countries viewed the United States and its policies on terrorism, the Middle East, Islam, oil, and the use of American military power in Muslim countries. In the four countries large majorities have negative views of the U.S. government, ranging from two-thirds in Indonesia and Pakistan to three-fourths in Morocco, and more than 90 percent in Egypt. Majorities in the four countries said the United States influences "most" or "nearly all" of what happens in the world (89 percent in Egypt said this). Other public opinion surveys in the past three years have also shown that Muslim negative perceptions of the United States have largely developed since 9/11 and focus principally on the Bush administration. Very large majorities (ranging from three-fourths in three of the countries to more than 90 percent in Egypt) believed the United States seeks to undermine Islam; majorities in these countries also believed that the United States seeks to weaken Islam "so that it will not grow and challenge the Western way of life." Almost two-thirds of respondents believed the United States "wanted to spread Christianity in the Middle East," and similar percentages also believed the United States' strategic goal is to "take advantage of the people of the Middle East" and guarantee access to oil, which they viewed as "illegitimate and exploitive."

The question on the U.S. war on terror elicited equally negative responses. When they were asked whether the primary goal of the war on terror was to "weaken and divide the Islamic religion and its people," "achieve political and military domination to control Middle East resources," or "protect itself from terrorist attacks," only very small minorities agreed with the third goal (ranging from 9 percent in Egypt to 23 percent in Indonesia). Large majorities in Morocco, Egypt, and Pakistan and more than half in Indonesia believed that weakening the Islamic world and achieving political and military domination were the two primary goals of the U.S.-led war on terror. To counter these views, American public diplomacy should be able to explain clearly and convincingly that the United States is not out to dominate or occupy the Muslim world, capture its resources, weaken the Muslim faith, or spread Christianity in Muslim lands.

Large majorities of respondents (ranging from almost two-thirds in Indonesia to more than 90 percent in Egypt) opposed the presence of U.S. troops in Muslim countries and endorsed the goal of removing American forces and bases from Muslim countries. Consistent with this position, majorities in Egypt and Morocco (more than 90 percent in Egypt and four out of five in Morocco) approved attacks on U.S. troops in Iraq and Afghanistan and in the Persian Gulf states because they viewed them as occupiers. Pakistani respondents were split on the issue, and almost 60 percent of Indonesians disapproved of such attacks. On the question of the Israeli-Palestinian conflict, here again the United States received low ratings for its perceived pro-Israel bias. Majorities in the four countries saw the United States as encouraging Israel to expand its territory, and no majority or plurality in any country believed that the United States was genuine in its pursuit of an independent and viable Palestinian state. More than 90 percent of Egyptians and two-thirds of Moroccans believed the United States was not genuine about the establishment of an independent Palestinian state, and two-thirds or more in the four countries (ranging from 65 percent in Indonesia and Pakistan to 95 percent in Egypt) agreed with the goal of "trying to push the United States to stop favoring Israel in its conflict with the Palestinians." In conversations over the years, several educated Islamic activists conceded that the United States has strong and deep relations with Israel (one activist described Israel as the "fifty-first state of the United States") but argued that such relations do not preclude the American government from taking an "evenhanded" approach to the conflict, which they said it should do.

Though critical of American foreign policy and supportive of removing U.S. forces from Muslim countries, large majorities in the four countries opposed attacks against civilians for political purposes and saw such attacks as contrary to Islam. On average, three-fourths of those interviewed said that attacks against civilians could not be justified for whatever reason, which is a clear rejection of Bin Ladin's claims that under certain conditions Islam justifies the killing of innocent civilians. When asked whether they agreed with the statement that Islam opposes such attacks despite al-Qaʻida's claim to the contrary, large majorities in the three countries agreed with the statement (four in five in Egypt and two-thirds in Morocco and Indonesia). Pakistanis, however, were much more hesitant, with 30 percent supporting the statement and 35 percent opposing it. Although a majority of Pakistanis saw attacks on innocent civilians as unjustified, they did not agree that it totally contradicted Islam. Majorities in the four countries also viewed attacks on civilian infrastructures, even if no civilians were killed, as completely unjustifiable; only 10 percent said such attacks could be justified. Similarly, majorities in all countries opposed attacks on American and European civilians, even if these civilians were working for American companies in Muslim countries. Despite their opposition to American foreign policy in the Muslim world, majorities in the four countries expressed strong opposition to attacks on American civilians wherever they are. The picture becomes more complex on the question of suicide attacks. Majorities in three countries said suicide attacks were rarely or never justified. Sixty percent of Egyptians, however, tended to believe that suicide attacks were sometimes or often justified. When asked whether they viewed terrorism as a problem, large majorities said they saw it as a problem or a very large problem. Furthermore, majorities in the four countries viewed the September 11 attacks as having been "negative for the people of the Islamic world." Here again, U.S. public diplomacy should capitalize on Muslim opposition to terrorism and devise themes that would appeal to Muslims.

Majorities or pluralities also opposed al-Qaʿidaʾs attacks on Americans, but many said they shared some of al-Qaʿidaʾs attitudes toward the United States. Perhaps the most significant finding of the survey, however, was that majorities or large majorities in the four countries endorsed six goals, which they also believed were goals of al-Qaʿida. Their strong or somewhat strong endorsement of these goals was not deterred by the fact that these same goals were espoused by al-Qaʿida and like-minded radical organizations. The six goals were "to push the United States to stop favoring Israel in its conflict with the Palestinians," "to keep Western values out of Islamic countries," "to stand up to America and affirm the dignity of the Islamic people," "to push the United States to remove its military bases from all Islamic countries," "to require a strict application of Sharia in every Islamic country," and "to unify all Islamic countries into a single Islamic state or Caliphate." Although the goal about establishing a caliphate might threaten the stability of Muslim governments, the majority of respondents perhaps viewed the attainment of this goal as a way to strengthen the Muslim world and recapture lost glories of Islamic civilization.

On the other hand, large majorities in the four countries had a positive view of globalization (greater connectivity through trade and communication) and endorsed democracy "as a good way of governing their country." When asked whether violent conflict between Muslim and Western cultures was inevitable or whether it was possible to find common ground, majorities in Indonesia and Morocco and pluralities in Egypt and Pakistan rejected the notion of inevitable conflict and expressed the belief that common ground could be found between Western and Muslim cultures. This finding was corroborated in a BBC World Service poll conducted in early 2007 in twenty-seven countries, which found that a majority of those polled said they saw positive links between Muslim and Western cultures and that the conflict between cultures was politically motivated, not a clash of civilizations. One activist, repeating an earlier call by former Iranian president Muhammad Khatami, said, "We and the West should pursue a dialogue of cultures, not a clash of civilizations."

The low standing of the United States in the Muslim world since 9/11 is equally evident in a series of surveys conducted by the Pew Global Attitudes Project (pewglobal.org). As was pointed out in other polls, negative attitudes toward the United States reflected criticism of policies on several issues: invading Iraq and Afghanistan; rejection of Hamas's electoral victory; a bellicose posture toward Iran; strong support for Israel and acquiescence in its war against Lebanon in the summer of 2006; tepid commitment to democratic ideals of good governance and a two-state solution in Palestine; and working with authoritarian regimes. A 2006 fifteen-nation Pew survey showed that the favorability ratings of the United States continued to slip in the past half-dozen years in Muslim and non-Muslim countries. For example, between 2002 and 2006, favorable opinions of the United States went down in Great Britain (75 to 56 percent), France (63 to 39 percent), Germany (61 to 37 percent), Spain (38 to 23 percent), Russia (61 to 43 percent), and Japan (72 to 63 percent). In selected Muslim countries where data are available, American rankings were much lower. In Indonesia, favorable opinion of the United States declined from 61 to 30 percent (despite the tsunami aid that the United States provided to that country in 2005). Turkey saw a decline from 30 to 15 percent, and Jordan from 25 to 15 percent. America's image also declined between 2005 and 2006 in India (71 to 56 percent) and in Indonesia (38 to 30 percent).

Muslim nations generally did not share the concerns of the United States and some of its European allies over Iran's nuclear threat and Hamas's electoral victory; large majorities of Muslims, according to the 2006 Pew poll, felt that the Hamas victory was good for the Palestinian people: 87 percent in Pakistan, 76 percent in Egypt, 68 percent in Jordan, and 61 percent in Indonesia. Many Muslim interlocutors and newspaper articles have argued that the U.S. failure to find weapons of mass destruction in Iraq, despite former Secretary of State Colin Powell's impassioned speech to the United Nations, has significantly undermined the credibility of American warnings about Iran's nuclear program. Furthermore, some of the interlocutors told me that Muslim Iran should have the right to have nuclear weapons in a region where Israel is the only nuclear power. "Why focus on Iran and not on Israel?" another interlocutor insisted.

The 2006 survey showed that international support for the U.S.-led war on terror has declined and that the Iraq war continues to drag America's image down; in ten of fourteen European and Muslim countries surveyed, majorities or large pluralities said that the world is a more dangerous place because of the Iraq war: 56 percent in Spain, 60 percent in Great Britain, 56 percent in Egypt, 58 percent in Jordan, and 60 percent in Turkey. According to the Pew poll, confidence in President Bush's ability to do the right thing has declined significantly from 2003 to 2006 in European and Muslim countries: from 51 to percent in Great Britain, 33 to 25 percent in Germany, 20 to 15 percent in France, 26 to 7 percent in Spain, and 8 to 3 percent in Turkey. His favorability ratings in 2006 were very low in Pakistan (10 percent), Jordan (7 percent), and Egypt (8 percent). Bush was viewed in many countries, according to the Pew surveys, as the principal cause of what is wrong with the United States and with American policy. In the same survey, majorities and large majorities in Indonesia, Pakistan, Turkey, Jordan, and Lebanon said that they were very or somewhat worried that the United States could be a military threat to their country. The Israeli war against Lebanon in the summer of 2006 confirmed the fears of many Lebanese about potential American threats to their country. Concerns over the U.S. war in Iraq were also evident in the 2006 survey. Majorities and large majorities in almost all countries surveyed said that the invasion of Iraq and removal of Saddam Hussein have made the world more dangerous. More than 60 percent in European countries and Japan and more than 70 percent in Jordan, Turkey, and Egypt agreed with this position. Pluralities, majorities, and large majorities also said that efforts to establish democracy in Iraq will fail.

Many Muslim interlocutors revealed a sense of bewilderment as to why the United States has not been able to do better in its relations with the Muslim world. An Indonesian Muslim asked, perhaps rhetorically, "Does America really care about what we think?" I recalled the question two years later in 2005 when a senior NSC official asked me to get involved in a "new" and "more vigorous" Muslim outreach program. In fact, I asked the same official "whether we really cared about what the Muslim world thought of us." If we did not care, which would be shortsighted and not in the best interest of the United States, we should abandon all public diplomacy attempts at reaching out to Muslim peoples. "If we cared, because our national security demands it, then we should embark on a major, national effort to repair our relations with the Muslim world." He said, "Of course, we cared." Public opinion polls continue to show that three years later not much has been done to improve America's low standing across the Muslim world. The analysis in the next five sections focuses on major policy areas that my Muslim interlocutors identified as troublesome, and as the polls have shown, these concerns are also shared by majorities and large pluralities in non-Muslim countries, including America's traditional allies in Western Europe. If the United States hopes to develop an effective public diplomacy campaign to win the hearts and minds of Arabs and Muslims, it is imperative to understand the issues and concerns that many Muslims have raised. These policy issues, ranging from the war on terror to American unilateralism in foreign relations, constitute the foundation of the blueprint for public diplomacy discussed in the next chapter. No public diplomacy could be considered credible unless U.S. policymakers assess these issues in light of the country's strategic interests and then apply their findings with conviction through a robust public diplomacy process.

GLOBAL WAR ON TERROR

Seven years after 9/11, the global war on terror and the commitment of enormous American resources in manpower and treasure in pursuit of that "war" have not made Americans measurably safer than they were on the eve of the terrorist attacks in New York and Washington. As the memory of the 9/11 tragedy fades from people's memories and as the top leaders of al-Qaʿida remain free or easily replaced, Muslims and others are questioning the execution, success, and future direction of this "war." Official and media reports and a recently declassified National Intelligence Estimate (NIE) have all indicated that al-Qaʿida has regained its strength and operational capabilities and now poses a growing threat to the United States. According to the declassified Key Judgments of the July 2007 NIE, the intelligence community now assesses that al-Qaʿida and its affiliates and like-minded organizations will remain "a persistent and evolving terrorist threat over the next three years" to the United States. The "global" war is rapidly becoming an American effort, and the intelligence community is concerned that the level of international cooperation that existed right after 2001 "may wane as 9/11 becomes a more distant memory and perceptions of threat diverge."

The NIE, which reflects the collective analytic assessment of the sixteen intelligence entities in the U.S. government, offered several other sobering judgments: al-Qaʿida remains the "most serious threat" to the nation, and "its central leadership continues to plan high-impact plots"; it has "protected or regenerated key elements" of its capability to strike the United States, including a safe haven in Pakistan's frontier tribal areas (known as the Federally Administered Tribal Areas or FATA), operational leaders, and its top leadership; and al-Qaʿida's association with like-minded groups in Iraq is energizing its recruiting efforts, indoctrination effectiveness, and fundraising. Obviously, while the invasion of Afghanistan forced al-Qaʿida and its allies the Taliban out of that country, it failed to eliminate either group; on the contrary, both groups have gotten stronger and are posing a real threat to the Karzai regime in Afghanistan and the government in Pakistan. Similarly, the invasion of Iraq and the removal of Saddam Hussein have created a fertile ground for al-Qaʿida and other radical Sunni organizations, something that did not exist in Iraq before the invasion. Contrary to persistent administration claims over the past four years that Iraq poses a serious terrorist threat to the United States, public statements by the intelligence community now maintain that the principal terrorist threat lies not in Iraq but in South Asia, a situation that prevailed on the eve of 9/11.

Furthermore, the NIE assesses that al-Qaʿida remains intent on acquiring and employing weapons of mass destruction in future attacks and once it has the capability, it would not hesitate to use such materials. Accordingly, the NIE assesses that the "the United States is in a heightened threat environment." Because of the growing capability of al-Qaʿida in recent years and the continued survival of its top leaders, the spread of radical ideology, which has been greatly enhanced through the Internet and other tools and forums of electronic communication, has become much more energized and will remain so for the next three years. Virtual jihadist ideology has become a potent dual agent of proselytization and recruitment. The fact that al-Qaʿida top leaders, especially Usama Bin Ladin and his deputy Ayman al-Zawahiri, are alive and capable of communicating messages and operational plans to their followers signals to radical jihadists and potential recruits that the United States has failed to defeat al-Qaʿida. Whenever Bin Ladin or al-Zawahiri issues an audio or a video statement, the symbolism of their continued ability to record and produce sophisticated tapes or DVDs is not lost on their followers and future recruits. A Muslim activist asked, "If Bin Ladin and Zawahiri are living in the caves and on the run, how can they produce such sophisticated tapes even with English subtitles?" It is an interesting point to ponder as al-Qaʿida media production arm, al-Sahab Media, remains in the information business. Whenever Bin Ladin or Zawahiri issues a new message, he gains points in his propaganda war against the West by showing his followers that he is still alive. To many Muslim high school students and potential jihadist recruits, al-Qaʿidaʾs leadership ability to elude the capture and the sophisticated tracking by American intelligence and military is a sign that "God is on Bin Ladinʾs side!" Of course, the average Muslim is not convinced by the American argument that capturing one or two men in remote areas of South Asia is almost an impossible task; on the contrary, he views this fact as a sign of American weakness and Muslim strength.

At least three perceptions of the U.S.-led global war on terror drive Islamic negative views of this war: the war is principally a unilateral American project, not a global enterprise that could relate to the interests of other states; the United States has prosecuted the war on terror through a concerted anti-Arab and anti-Muslim political posture; and the United States has painted all Muslims with the same broad brush without any distinction between mainstream or centrist Islamic activists and radical or jihadist Muslims. Muslim interlocutors repeatedly told me that "in the eyes of America all Muslims are suspect," even though many Muslims have renounced terrorism and al-Qaʿida. An Islamic activist who had studied in the United States added, "By lumping all of us together and considering all of us potential terrorists, your government has discredited Islamic liberals and reformers and enhanced the stature of radicals. Itʾs as if we are all guilty until proven innocent!" The educational and travel plans of many Muslim college and university students who wanted to study in the United States were interrupted because they could not get a visa, or because they were detained and sent back to their countries, or because they were singled out and harassed at the points of entry. Consequently, many Muslim students canceled their long-term plans to study in the United States.

Furthermore, many Muslims have been angered by the fact that the war on terror has led the United States to cooperate closely with intelligence services in other countries, oftentimes against citizens of those countries, which inevitably resulted in human rights abuses that the American government seemed to condone. Stories of detention centers and interrogation prisons at Abu Ghraib, Guantanamo, and in Europe and Middle Eastern countries have been widely disseminated in Arab and Islamic media throughout the Muslim world and Europe, leading many Muslims to question the United States' commitment to human rights, justice, and the rule of law. The United States has been accused of condoning regime repression of dissidents, even secular, liberal dissidents, in the name of fighting terrorism. According to academic research, pro-reform activists also have been critical of the global war on terror because it allowed many regimes to restrict the activities of civil society institutions and deny them the right to organize politically and field candidates in national elections. Civil society activists cite Egypt, Jordan, Bahrain, Morocco, Yemen, the Palestinian Authority, Algeria, and Tunisia as examples of countries whose repressive measures against dissidents have been tolerated by the United States as a price those regimes have exacted for their cooperation on counterterrorism. Academic experts also argue that by taking a Manichaean approach to fighting terrorism—you are either with us or against us—American policymakers in effect have denied the centrist or *wasatiyya* groups, political parties, and civil society organizations a meaningful role in the political process in their respective countries, with the United States siding with regimes against all forms of opposition. An Egyptian civil society, pro-democracy activist described the global war on terror as a "struggle for the hearts and minds of authoritarian regimes who tell the Americans what they want to hear and who fill their pockets and the pockets of their family members and political cronies with millions of dollars, all in the name of fighting terrorism. If the Americans dare to object to flagrant human rights abuses, the regime tells them not to interfere in the internal affairs of a sovereign nation!"

According to Arab human rights advocates, Muslims who

oppose terrorism see the cooperation between the United States
and Western intelligence services as a legitimate method of obtaining and sharing information in the pursuit of terrorists, but
by cooperating with Arab and Muslim security and intelligence
services, the United States is seen as condoning human rights
violations, arrests without charges, harsh interrogations, and
even torture. A Muslim activist said to me, "When your government sends people to some Arab countries for interrogation, do
you think Egyptian or Jordanian intelligence obtains information from these jihadists by feeding them hummus and baklava?
Of course, they torture them." In his mind and the minds of
many others like him, such American phrases as "enhanced interrogation techniques" are a euphemism for torture. This activist said that the claims repeatedly made by American policymakers that they did not know what other countries did with
Muslim prisoners "does not absolve your government of torture." U.S. public diplomacy needs to underscore a central point
of the "war on terror"—namely, that the United States together
with other Muslim and non-Muslim states aims at targeting terrorist criminals who have killed innocent civilians, violated national and international norms, and corrupted the teachings of
Islam. Public diplomacy also needs to point out that tracking
Islamic terrorists is not a war against Islam and that Muslims,
both Sunni and Shia, have suffered even more casualties at the
hands of terrorists than the United States has. The United States
should signal its intensions to investigate those policy areas that
have been identified by public opinion polls as problematic for
Muslim publics.

INVADING MUSLIM COUNTRIES

The U.S.-led invasion of Iraq, the continued occupation of that
country, and the high toll of Iraqi civilians have severely diminished America's standing in the Arab Islamic world, according
to Arab media and public opinion polls. American public diplomacy has suffered from what Muslims see as a trigger-happy
approach to problems in the Muslim world, which began with
the invasion of Afghanistan right after 9/11. Islamic activists

view the Iraq invasion as a twenty-first-century colonial war by the United States designed to effect regime change and to dominate Arab and Muslim countries either directly or by proxy. Numerous Arab and Islamic media reports and analyses have alleged that U.S. policy to undermine Hamas's elected government, America's acquiescence in the Israeli war in Lebanon in the summer of 2006, and Washington's saber rattling against Iran provided further evidence of United States' anti-Arab and anti-Islamic policy. When it comes to Arabs and Muslims, many Islamic activists believe that American policy seems to promote the use of force or the threat to use force as a first resort. An Arab journalist told me on a trip to the Middle East, "You could never have good relations with the Middle East if you base your policy on a cowboy mentality of shoot first and ask questions later!" Many Arabs and Muslims (and others for that matter) believe that the Iraq war was unnecessary, that Saddam was contained through a tough sanctions regime, that the United States went to war on false premises, and that regime change rather than disarming Saddam was the real goal of the war. They also believe that the U.S. failure to secure Iraq after toppling the regime has unleashed a bloody sectarian violence that will threaten the region for years to come, and Iraqi instability will embolden Iran to expand its regional influence and undermine the stability of neighboring Sunni Arab regimes. Arabs and Sunni Muslims place the blame for the chaos and bloodshed in Iraq and for the growing sectarianism across the region squarely on the shoulders of the United States.

Public opinion polls have shown that the United States seems to pursue its interests with swagger and arrogance and little or no empathy for the concerns of peoples around the world. Polling data have also shown that the unilateral use of force as a tool of American foreign policy since 9/11 has damaged the country's ability to manage its relations with Arabs and Muslims through diplomacy. The United States should revisit this issue and explore tangible ways to restore America's good standing through diplomacy, not war. What is most disturbing about the polls and my interviews with Arabs and Muslims is that the United States seems unable or unwilling to communicate with peoples and continues to back governments and regimes that have lost the confidence of their people and that cling to power through repression, corruption, mismanagement, and reliance on their security services and foreign, invariably U.S., support. As a strategic foreign policy goal, democratization and political reform require a new foreign policy based on engaging civil society groups and organizations. A creative public diplomacy is the first step to initiate such engagement.

Public opinion polls have indicated that two major unintended consequences have resulted from America's recent wars in Muslim lands: increased terrorism and deepening sectarianism. Before the war, al-Qa'ida abhorred Iraq's Ba'thist secular ideology, but after the invasion al-Qa'ida declared Iraq a legitimate battleground for jihad against the "Crusaders" and began to call on jihadists to go to Iraq. "Al-Qa'ida in Iraq" was established and became the spearhead of the Sunni insurgency and anti-Shia violence. Recruits, resources, and weapons poured into Iraq, and suicide bombings became the weapon of choice of the insurgents. Al-Qa'ida Iraq has no shortage of recruits or leaders. Although organized Islamic activism and radicalism were banned during the Saddam era, the invasion changed all that, and, according to numerous academic experts, Iraq is on the verge of becoming a failed state run by militias and sectarian centers of power. The secularism that characterized the brutal Saddam regime and the sense of equality that many educated Iraqi women felt during the Saddam era have been replaced by a conservative, narrow-minded Islamic ideology on both sides of the Sunni-Shia divide. These same experts argued that Saddam's tyranny has been replaced by uncontrollable chaos, leading some to speculate that democracy is a lost cause and that what Iraq needs is another dictator to reestablish law and order. Should this come to pass, it will be the ultimate proof of the utter failure of the American project in Iraq, leading Muslims and non-Muslims to conclude that thousands of Iraqis and Americans have died in vain and that the so-called shining beacon of Iraqi democracy is nothing more than a mirage evaporated on the sand dunes of the Iraqi desert. The war planners in Washington perhaps were clear on what they wanted Iraq and the greater Middle East to look like after 2003, but they certainly had a clouded vision of the realities on the ground and finally lost their way in the darkness of the *khamsin* winds and the sand storms. Afghanistan has also seen a resurgence of Taliban and al-Qaʿida terrorism since the U.S.-led invasion in 2001. In parts of Afghanistan today, government authority does not exist, and some villages have barely noticed that the Taliban are no longer in power. Some Afghans frequently referred to President Hamid Karzai as the "Mayor of Kabul" to denote his limited authority throughout the country. On a visit to Kandahar in southeastern Afghanistan in the fall of 2003, I got the clear impression that religious leaders with Taliban sympathies were the source of authority and symbol of power in that area, and government presence was not evident outside that city. I interviewed a leading cleric in Kandahar who had written against terrorism and who forcefully urged his Pashtun followers to reject terrorism and the Taliban. He told me he was taking a big risk in speaking out against al-Qaʿida, particularly in the Kandahar area, where many people do not recognize the regime in Kabul. Unfortunately, his fears came true; he was assassinated a few months later. The situation has gotten much worse since then. In the summer of 2007, the intelligence community publicly identified the Afghan-Pakistan border areas as the center of gravity of serious terrorist threats against the United States. Whereas before 2001 we faced a single terrorist front, mainly in Afghanistan, seven years later al-Qaʿida and its affiliates are operating out of two fronts (Iraq and Afghanistan) simultaneously. Arabs and Muslims blame the United States for inadvertently creating the new situation, prompting many Americans and others to say they feel less safe now than before 9/11. Although it is possible to argue that the Karzai government might have more legitimacy than the Iraqi government, Afghanistan lacks the resources to build a viable country. Policymakers need to take a strategic and dispassionate look at what has led to the collapse of these two states and devise corrective policies. Only then can a forward-looking sustainable public diplomacy emerge.

Shia-Sunni sectarianism has been the other destructive by-product of the Iraq war. The sectarian violence that has been unleashed in Iraq, claiming thousands of casualties, has for all intents and purposes ruined and dismembered the Iraqi state, destroyed the personal security of individual Iraqis, and now threatens to spread to other parts of the Middle East and South Asia. Sectarianism is no longer just a "high politics" problem; it has left a bloody trail in local neighborhoods and turned members of the same family against each other. Sectarianism in Iraq has deprived individuals and groups of the ability to pursue their daily lives, inside and outside their homes, without fear of intimidation, kidnapping, loss of property, assassination, or death. It has prevented many Iraqis from seeking and holding a job and forced them to leave their homes and live as refugees in Iraq and elsewhere. Sectarian violence, like terrorism, is also blamed on the United States and has contributed to low favorability ratings of America, and the Bush administration in particular, in public opinion polls. Sectarianism has also created an uproar among Sunni activists throughout the region against the perceived mistreatment of Iraqi Sunnis and the role of a resurgent Iran in fueling Shia empowerment. Despite almost five years of occupation, billions of dollars spent, and thousands of U.S. and Iraqi casualties, the growing irrelevance of external actors to Iraqi instability clearly indicates that the primary responsibility of security in Iraq and of the future of Iraq—as a unified, viable state or a partitioned, failed state—rests primarily on Iraqis and secondarily on their neighbors. The lofty plans of restructuring Iraqi society from within through a liberal, democratic, and inclusive political and social system that were enunciated with the start of the war in the spring of 2003 have all but dissipated because of ongoing sectarian violence. Like other Arabs and Muslims, more and more Iraqis from all walks of life are openly placing the blame for such violence and instability squarely on the United States.

The other negative by-product of the Iraq war is the huge refugee problem involving millions of Iraqis who fled from their homes to other areas within the country or who had the financial means and connections to flee to neighboring countries, especially Jordan and Syria. The long-term impact of the Iraqi refugee problem on neighboring states and on future American policy toward the region remains to be addressed, and a solution is a prerequisite for crafting a new public diplomacy targeting Arabs and Muslims. It is equally imperative to engage Syria and Jordan on this issue in order to alleviate the suffering of the refugees, to help the host states cope with the influx of hundreds of thousands of Iraqis, and ultimately to foster an environment in Iraq that would entice Iraqis to return to their homeland and start a process of national reconciliation. Syria and Jordan find themselves burdened with the refugee problem on top of the other decades-old problem of Palestinian refugees. What is most disturbing for the future of Iraq is that because so many affluent and professional Iraqis have left the country, the population that is left behind is becoming poorer, less educated, less professional, and more sectarian. Here again, many Sunni Muslims blame the United Stated for the changing demography and growing sectarianism of Iraq.

Beyond Iraq and Afghanistan, Arab Islamic activists in 2006–7 pointed to two other examples of American bellicosity in the Middle East—acquiescence in the massive Israeli air strikes against Lebanon in order to destroy Hizballah, and heightened rhetoric against Iran in response to that country's nuclear program and its increasing support of the Iraqi insurgency. Arab commentators and media have described the Lebanon war as the "sixth Arab-Israeli war," and have pointed out that unlike previous wars where the United States played a key role in ending them, especially in 1967 and 1973, this time, in their view, the United States prolonged the war, giving Israel more time against Hizballah. Some Arab and Muslim commentators and activists have claimed that American military and political support of Israel in the summer war aimed at helping Israel defeat an Arab "resistance" force, and the longer Hizballah withstood the Israeli military assault, the more frustrated Israel and the United States became. These commentators have also maintained that had the United States been seriously interested in ending the war, the cease-fire formula that was adopted several weeks after the war started could have been achieved three or four weeks into the war. Regarding Iran, critics maintained that the United States was setting the stage to attack Iran with an eye toward changing the clerical regime in Tehran. In the words of one Islamic activist, "Should that happen, it would be the fifth in a series of American aggressive acts against the Muslim world; the other four being Afghanistan, Iraq, Lebanon, and Hamas." In all five, according to this reasoning, regime change was always the goal. An Arab interlocutor told me, "the Taliban are gone, Saddam is gone, Hamas is on a life-support system, and the Ayatollahs are next." It would be a tall order to disabuse such critics of the notion that the United States does not intend to conquer the Islamic world and remove Muslim regimes that do not hue the American line.

DEMOCRATIZATION

Arab and Muslim pro-democracy activists have viewed American commitment to democratization in Arab and Muslim countries as vacillating and confused, leading many of them to question American sincerity and the veracity of its lofty rhetoric on the issue. According to Muslim interlocutors and public opinion polls, the perceived American vacillation on democratization has undercut the United States image among Arabs and Muslims and dramatically weakened its engagement with the Muslim world. A secular Arab interlocutor asked, "If the United States cannot stand up for genuine democracy, what can you stand for?" Several factors contributed to the erosion of American credibility on the question of democracy in the Arab Muslim world. The pro-democracy speeches that President Bush gave in 2002 and 2003 resonated well among Arab secular elites and Islamic activists, but the bounce from those speeches lasted only a short time because the speeches were not followed by tangible programs. In addition, authoritarian regimes from Egypt to Uzbekistan objected strongly to the democracy initiative on the grounds that democracy breeds instability, and despite high-level American speeches, these regimes maintained business-as-usual regarding popular participation in decision making and continued to engage in cosmetic elections as a superficial way to enhance their legitimacy. According to CIA director Tenet, the United States equated democracy with elections but paid little attention to civil society institutions and spent minimal resources on nurturing a culture of democracy in those countries. Arab elites welcomed the president's speeches but regimes paid only scant attention to them, and radical Islamic activists including al-Qaʿida accused the United States of imposing its version of democracy on Arab and Muslim countries.

Regimes rejected American calls for democracy as an imposition from the outside, al-Qaʿida renounced American calls for democracy as an attempt to undermine Islamic values, and secular elites criticized the American rhetoric as superficial because, while calling for democracy, the United States in their view continued to coddle authoritarian regimes and accept their version of what is best for their countries. Arab analysts also have criticized the United States for not objecting forcefully to regimes' pernicious schemes to control the elections and fraudulently orchestrate election results in advance. Civil society institutions in Egypt, Jordan, Syria, Tunisia, and elsewhere were energized by the American call for democracy and spent much effort and time in educating their publics and preparing their societies for democracy. However, when they began to speak on behalf of human rights, field candidates, campaign openly against the unbridled authoritarianism of their regimes, demand that outside observers supervise the election against potential regime abuse, and work with international human rights and other NGOs to facilitate the process of democracy, regimes reacted harshly and virtually shut down the process. Several pro-democracy advocates were harassed, jailed, and accused of working with and receiving money from foreign entities, and they quickly discovered that they could not stand up to their powerful regimes, especially as they felt they could not rely on the United States for help. Islamic political parties were often banned from participating or controlled by the regime, and when they did participate, regimes played the sectarian card to divide the Islamic vote. Civil society institutions sought assistance from the United States in their struggle for democracy, which, as one secular activist put it, "was a strategic goal of the

American government," but the American government did very little to control regime manipulation of the electoral process. Secular and Islamic pro-democracy activists began to accuse the United States government of hypocrisy and expediency. Another activist described the entire American approach to democracy as a "sham."

According to major newspapers in the region, the Bush administration's hostile reaction to Hamas's victory at the polls in 2006 was perhaps the most critical factor that undercut American public diplomacy on the issue of democracy. In order to showcase its democracy project in the Arab world, the Bush administration strongly supported the holding of Palestinian national elections, and, though unexpected, Palestinians welcomed Hamas's electoral victory as a repudiation of the Palestinian Authority's mismanagement, corruption, nepotism, and generally poor governance. Hamas was not elected because of its emphasis on *Sharia* or Islamic law, but because of the party's perceived honesty, service to the community, and nationalist credentials, especially its struggle against the Israeli occupation. The United States and Israel denounced the election results, refused to recognize the Hamas-led government despite its legitimacy under Palestinian law, and withheld aid and other funds from the new government. Arab and Muslim reaction was swift in denouncing the American position as a violation of democratic principles and people's right to vote. A Muslim contact described the American posture as "support for selective democracy." He said, "America supports elections only if it likes the results." According to public opinion polls and many Muslim interlocutors, the favorability ratings of the United States plummeted because of Washington's Hamas policy, which they believed was symptomatic of America's refusal to accept mainstream centrist Islamic political parties as legitimate players in the political process. Another Islamic activist asked, "How can you embark on political reform in Muslim countries without engaging Islamic political parties?" The Hamas victory was followed by a successful election involving the Muslim Brotherhood in Egypt and the Shia Wifaq Party in Bahrain. Although people vote for Islamic parties for different reasons, the fact remains that in Muslim countries Islamic political parties are expected to participate in national elections and be actively involved in the governing process; they are also expected to do well in elections that are free and fair.

The electoral victory of the Justice and Development Party (AKP) in Turkey's legislative elections and its ability to form a single-party government offer another example of a centrist Islamic party coming to power in a traditionally Muslim country and a useful model for engaging Muslim parties in governance. Islamic parties need not be a threat just because of their Islamic roots; in fact, their legislative behavior in government after they come to power, not their ideology, should be the metric by which they should be judged. By returning the party to power, a majority of Turkish voters signaled their support of the party's performance, indicating their confidence that AKP would guard the country's secular culture and would continue to push for membership in the European Community. The Turkish electorate also seemed comfortable with AKP's Islamic roots and did not see any inherent contradiction between the party's Islamic ideology and the future of Turkey as a modern state. By electing AKP, the Turkish people have indicated they no longer viewed the Turkish military as the praetorian guard of secularism or Kemalism in Turkey, a role that the military assigned to itself for more than eighty years. The electorate did not heed the warnings voiced by the military on the eve of the election of dire consequences if AKP is returned to parliament with a majority. The electorate emphatically told the military that a duly elected civilian leadership, even if it espouses an Islamic ideology, could be trusted with protecting the nation's heritage, and the military's proper place is in the barracks, not in politics.

Herein lies a most significant lesson for other militaries in the region, from Egypt to Pakistan, and for the United States as well. If a centrist Islamic party could be trusted to do well in Turkey, why not explore similar possibilities in other Muslim countries? American policymakers should seriously analyze the success of AKP and encourage other Islamic political parties to emulate the Turkish nationalist-Islamic experience, keeping in mind, of course, the unique circumstances that prevail in different Muslim countries. The ideological divide that separates nationalist Islamic parties from al-Qaʿida and other radical groups is at the center of ongoing debate within Islam and could be exploited to involve these parties in the political process. Al-Qaʿida's strenuous and shrill objections to the participation of Islamic parties in elections, as demonstrated in several statements by Bin Ladin's deputy al-Zawahiri, has failed to dissuade these parties from participating in national elections, indicating that nationalist Islamic activism remains a potent force. The nature and long-term impact of this phenomenon could be used by U.S. policymakers as a vehicle to engage Islamic political parties. Not dealing with these parties is no longer tenable and in the long run will be harmful to American national security. As several of these parties have made a serious commitment to democracy and have shown a high degree of pragmatism and willingness to compromise with other centrist and secular groups, they should be welcomed as potentially credible partners in the political transformation of their societies.

THE ISRAELI-PALESTINIAN CONFLICT: AN "HONEST BROKER" ROLE?

Public opinion polls and interviews with Muslims in recent years have shown that perceived American pro-Israel bias in dealing with the Israeli-Palestinian conflict has contributed to the unfavorability ratings of the United States in the region. Equally important is the prevalent view among many Arabs and Muslims that the United States' role is critical for any movement toward removing the occupation and moving the parties to the negotiations table. American presidents over the years have called for a resolution of the conflict and spent time, effort, and resources to attain a just and fair peace. It is almost axiomatic that resolving the conflict is good for American national interest, for the two peoples involved, and for the Middle East region. As polling data have indicated, resolving the conflict will eliminate a major impediment on the road to Muslim world outreach and a powerful driver of terrorism in the region and beyond. In fact, almost every message that has come out of al-

Qaʿida in the past decade has mentioned the Israeli occupation of Palestine and Jerusalem and the plight of the Palestinian people under the decades-long occupation. Majorities of Muslims have signaled in their responses to public opinion surveys that they strongly favor a just and fair resolution of the conflict. Because of Jerusalem's importance for Muslims (Qurʾan, 17:1), which they consider third in importance after Mecca and Medina, the Israeli occupation of East Jerusalem is a cause célèbre for all Muslims regardless of how they feel about the Palestinians. The question of Jerusalem always came up in my conversations with Islamic activists in Nigeria, Indonesia, Malaysia, India, Kenya, Turkey, and all over the Middle East.

In 2006 the Baker-Hamilton Iraq Study Group (ISG) recommended, "There must be a renewed and sustained commitment by the United States to a comprehensive Arab-Israeli peace on all fronts: Lebanon and Syria, and President Bush's June 2002 commitment to a two-state solution for Israel and Palestine" (Recommendation 13). The ISG made a few important but all-too-obvious points: there is no military solution to the problem; a solution can come about only through direct talks involving the Israelis, the Palestinians, and the neighboring states; the United States is committed to the survival of Israel; and such a solution must be based on UN Security Council Resolutions 242 and 338 (land for peace). In Recommendation 17, the ISG said that a negotiated peace should include five key elements: "Adherence to UN Security Council Resolutions 242 and 338; strong support for Palestinian President Mahmoud Abbas and the Palestinian Authority to take the lead in preparing the way for negotiations with Israel; a major effort to move from the current hostilities by consolidating the cease-fire reached between the Palestinians and the Israelis in November 2006; support for a national unity government; and sustainable negotiations leading to a final peace settlement along the lines of President Bush's two-state solution, which would address the key final status issues of borders, settlements, Jerusalem, the right of return, and the end of conflict."

A year after the ISG issued its report, Palestinian internecine violence raged in Gaza between Fatah and Hamas, resulting in a humiliating defeat of Fatah forces, the dismantling of the Palestinian Authority's political structure and authority, and the fall of Gaza under the complete control of Hamas. The United States, Israel, and President Mahmoud Abbas denounced the Hamas takeover of Gaza, which Abbas described as a "coup," and both the United States and Israel quickly came to the aid of Abbas. By late summer 2007, Abbas, like many Palestinians in the West Bank and Gaza, realized that he could not move forward toward a political settlement with Israel or on the road to reconciliation among Palestinians without engaging Hamas. Palestinian analysts have argued that Washington's policy to shore up Abbas's authority in the West Bank at the expense of Hamas in the long run is detrimental to the Palestinian people, to regional stability, and to Israeli and American strategic interests in the region. Such policy, they maintain, will institutionalize the split between the West Bank and Gaza, will undermine the peace efforts between the two peoples, and will beget more violence and terrorism. While Arabs and Muslims accept America's deep support for Israel as an enduring fact, they look to the United States to demonstrate a renewed seriousness in pushing the two sides to the negotiation table, with the dual goal of guaranteeing Israel's security and ending the Israeli occupation and Jewish settlements from the occupied territories. A Palestinian human rights activist said, "We are not asking for the moon; all we ask is for the United States to implement its own policy pronouncements about a two-state solution and the UN Security Council resolutions 242 and 338, which it drafted and supported."

The underlying assumption in the ISG recommendation is that American engagement in the process as an honest broker is critical to resolving the conflict. The influence of the United States with both parties has been a mixed blessing in that it gives Islamic activists and Arab nationalists a reason, rightly or wrongly, to always criticize the United States whenever the peace process is halted or whenever violence erupts among Palestinians or between Palestinians and Israelis. According to polls, the American "evenhanded" and "honest broker" role that characterized U.S. policy on the Palestinian issue over the years has all but disappeared under the Bush administration, especially since 9/11. Large majorities of Arabs and Muslims in most recent polls have said United States' policy has not done enough to end the occupation, remove the settlements, or alleviate the hardships and suffering of the Palestinian people. The continuing conflict and the United States seeming acceptance of the Israeli position against negotiations of final-status issues (settlements, borders, Jerusalem, and refugees), according to polls and interviews, have contributed to a heightened threat of regional war and global terrorism. The official rhetoric from Washington advocating a two-state solution and the frequent trips by the secretary of state and other high-ranking officials to the region no longer suffice as indicators of America's commitment to the peace process. The new "shuttle diplomacy" does not evoke good memories in the region. As one Palestinian told me in reference to official visits, "They come, they go, and we are still here—check points, roadblocks, travel permits, and delays!"

Of course, ending the Israeli occupation will not eliminate terrorism from the region completely but will deprive al-Qaʿida and other radical groups of the "Palestinian card" as a jihadist recruiting tool. Even at the height of its struggle against the Israeli occupation, Hamas rejected al-Qaʿida's overtures, arguing that the Palestinian cause focused on ending the Israeli occupation and was not part of global jihad, underscoring once more the rising phenomenon of nationalist, not globalist, Islamic activism. Hamas also participated in national elections and agreed to form a unity government with Fatah despite opposition from al-Qaʿida. Responding to Washington's negative reaction to Hamas election, a Palestinian Islamic activist said almost in exasperation, "We participated in the elections, we rejected al-Qaʿida, we formed a national unity government, and we said we would uphold previous international agreements signed by the Palestinian Authority. What else do you want us to do?" It is time to explore ways to reengage in the search for peace, tangibly and forcefully.

UNILATERALISM RESONATES POORLY

Unilateralism and a reliance on the use of force at the expense of world diplomacy have been identified in public opinion polls and interviews with Islamic activists as reasons behind the low favorability ratings of the United States. These criticisms, which cut across European and Muslim countries, maintain that the Bush administration has pursued its war on terror and related foreign policy initiatives unilaterally, without much attention to international diplomacy or international agreements such as the Geneva Conventions. Reliance on force, or the threat to use force, has been the key component of American foreign policy, something that majorities or pluralities of those interviewed in the polls saw as dangerous. The polls give a perception that fighting terrorism has given the administration the freedom to follow international agreements selectively, implementing what fits and discarding others. At least four examples have been cited as contributing to poor American standing in the world. They include global warming and the Bush administration's refusal to endorse the Kyoto agreement; holding detainees at the Guantanamo U.S. military base; the Abu Ghraib abuses; and the secret interrogation centers across Europe, the Middle East, and elsewhere. The invasion of Iraq and the threat to use force against Iran are also cited by critics as additional examples of American unilateralism in world affairs. One gets the impression from polls and interviews on the issue of a unilateralist foreign policy that the world, especially European publics, would like to see the United States return to the fold of multilateral diplomacy and use the tools of diplomacy to defend itself. The deployment of overwhelming force to resolve disputes with other nations and groups might produce instant success and gratification but does not guarantee long-term security, either for the United States or globally.

The rise of nonstate actors and all kinds of shadowy groups in international affairs and the diversity and complexity of threats have made traditional state boundaries more vulnerable. As states search for new tools to engage these actors and groups, it becomes more urgent than ever to turn to collective diplomacy in the search for answers to new threats; and as terrorism and other threats become global and are linked across state lines, effective responses will by necessity require multilateral actions. Public opinion findings indicate that unilateral, force-based actions are no longer adequate. Multilateral cooperation will augment the international community's expertise and capability in facing new global threats and will make the world safer. Public opinion polls have also indicated that American unilateral military actions against groups and countries have made the world less safe. The universal support the United States received after 9/11 and the goodwill it garnered about its military action against the Taliban dissipated rapidly as the administration began to prepare for war in Iraq. Whereas the military operations in Afghanistan were considered by most of the international community as a legitimate response to the terrorist acts on 9/11, the invasion of Iraq was viewed as an unjustified war of choice. Instead of building a peaceful, pluralistic, and democratic Iraq, under occupation Iraq became a failed state and a source of regional instability and violence and a breeding ground for terrorism, sectarian killings, and a total breakdown of law and order. The Maliki government cannot exercise meaningful authority beyond the walls of the American enclave known as the Green Zone and cannot provide for the personal security of Iraqi citizens. Neighboring states are watching with apprehension the disintegration of the Iraqi state as a society and a body politic and are blaming the United States for this disaster.

The five policy areas—the global war on terror, the invasion of Muslim countries, democratization, the Israeli-Palestinian conflict, and unilateralism—illustrate at once the impact of 9/11 on the new behavior of the United States in the world arena in the new century, the negative global attitudes toward this behavior, and the need to design a creative public diplomacy blueprint to recapture America's traditional good standing globally. It is necessary to change the substance of existing policies and the means by which to implement them. The effort will be a long-term, generational process, in which the United States will have to exhibit much patience, sophistication, expertise, and willingness to engage others. A new attitude toward foreign relations need not be Pollyannaish; it must be grounded in realism and in America's ability to pursue the strategic objectives it sets up for itself as it seeks to recapture its rightful, but just, place in the world.

Chapter 4

PUBLIC DIPLOMACY: A BLUEPRINT

I will appoint a special envoy to the Organization of the
Islamic Conference. . . . Our special envoy will listen to and
learn from representatives from Muslim states and will share
with them America's views and values. This is an opportunity
for Americans to demonstrate to Muslim communities our
interest in respectful dialogue and continued friendship.
—*President George W. Bush, speaking at the Islamic Center of
Washington, D.C., June 27, 2007*

I will also launch a program of public diplomacy that is a
coordinated effort across my Administration, not a small
group of political officials at the State Department
explaining a misguided war. We will open "America
Houses" in cities across the Islamic world. . . . I will make
clear that we are not at war with Islam.
—*Senator Barak Obama, speaking at the Wilson Center in
Washington, D.C., August 1, 2007*

NUMEROUS GOVERNMENT and private-sector reports and
speeches in the past six years have argued that American public
diplomacy in the Islamic World needs to be revamped. These
reports, together with polling data cited in the previous chapter,
have also urged that a new and a more effective public policy
approach be taken toward the Muslim world. This subject was
briefed on numerous occasions to the executive and legislative
branches of the government and to the Commission of the Intelligence Capabilities of the United States Regarding Weapons
of Mass Destruction (otherwise known as the WMD Commission). Right after 9/11 the author and another colleague represented the CIA for more than two years at an NSC interagency

working group on public diplomacy and Muslim world outreach. The underlying assumption of all public diplomacy efforts, statements, and reports in this period was that radicals and terrorists represented a small minority of Muslims and that the vast majority of Muslims tend to espouse moderate and tolerant views and do not engage in violent jihad. The often repeated phrase in the halls of official Washington in the early years after 9/11 was that the radicals represented 2 percent of Muslims, and the "moderates" represented the other 98 percent. Although the administration vigorously pursued the 2 percent, experts urged policymakers to reach out to the 98 percent of Muslims.

Understandably, in the immediate aftermath of 9/11, the focus was on the terrorists and whether they were planning to strike again and when. Media reports indicated that the government was totally absorbed with counterterrorism and saw no urgency to expend time and resources on Muslim world outreach. However, as months and years passed without another major terrorist strike against the United States, the intelligence community began to suggest that the U.S. government needed to learn more about the Muslim world and Islamic ideologies. Public diplomacy officials at the State Department wanted to know which Muslim 'ulama would be receptive to overtures from the United States, what American overtures would resonate with Muslims, and how to direct specific messages to specific audiences. By pursuing such an approach, State Department officials indicated, the American government would be in a much better position to persuade a majority of Muslims that military strikes against terrorists in Afghanistan or elsewhere were not a war on Islam and that terrorism is as much of a threat to Muslims as to non-Muslims. Some senior policymakers concurred with this view and began to push for a comprehensive public diplomacy initiative under the auspices of the NSC, not the State Department, which traditionally has managed public diplomacy. In the initial weeks, the working group met almost daily, then weekly, but disagreements began to emerge over who had the authority and capability to manage public diplomacy and to direct programs agreeable to the administration.

Public diplomacy and the "hearts and minds" campaigns initially centered on Afghanistan were a year and a half later diverted to Iraq. Despite the lofty rhetoric about the so-called 98 percent approach, no major initiatives were undertaken toward the Muslim world. The strategic goal of a successful public diplomacy campaign, as emerged in those discussions, must focus on reaching the 98 percent of Muslims, but even policymakers who were sympathetic to this position realized early on that it was much more difficult to accomplish because of the high degree of diversity among Muslims. Because of differences in ideology, religious practices, sectarianism, geography, demography, gender, ethnicity, race, age, education, culture, and language; the multiple audiences that exist in the Muslim world require a variety of messages to reach them. Recognizing that the Muslims of Indonesia, Egypt, Saudi Arabia, Uzbekistan, and Nigeria, for example, shared different cultural heritages and historical experiences and had diverse views of Islam and the role of Islam in society, American policymakers quickly abandoned a "one size fits all" message in favor of tailor-made messages targeting specific audiences. They also knew that messages were understood in terms of substance (what the message contains) and symbolism (how the message is worded and how it is delivered). Words are very important, especially for Arab and Muslim audiences, because of the rich oral tradition of the Qur'an. We all recall the furor that erupted throughout the Arab Muslim world in reaction to President Bush's use of the word "Crusade" in one of his speeches right after 9/11 about the war on terror. Many Arabs and Muslims focused on that particular word because it evoked an image of the Crusaders' invasion and occupation of Jerusalem and other Muslim lands and the Christian religious zeal that underpinned the Crusaders' war on Islam. Despite the administration's mea culpa, many Arab and Muslim commentators and journalists described the American-led invasion and occupation of Iraq as another "Crusader" war.

Knowing the educational level of the target audience definitely helps in honing the message and rendering it more effective. For years, the United States has reached out to college- and university-educated elites and professionals (mostly Western-educated, English-speaking, Scotch-drinking Muslims), but

Muslim populations today are becoming younger, less educated, more pious, poorer, and less able or inclined to travel to Western countries. While the elites in Muslim societies remain very important and must be engaged, we must reach out to those other millions who in many cases are unemployed, alienated, frustrated, and angry at their lot in life and at their governments. As jihadist recruits or foot soldiers frequently come from among these segments of the population, it is imperative, as many reports and briefings have indicated, that a public message of hope and opportunity reaches this youthful segment before it is radicalized. To do that, we must be clear on what the message is, which audiences it is supposed to address, and for what purpose. Targeting terrorism and terrorists is a short-term challenge that can best be approached as a law enforcement issue, and terrorists should be pursued and prosecuted as criminals. However, understanding and deciphering the societal context of Muslim communities in which terrorists and radicals operate is a long-term challenge that requires deep expertise, sophisticated analytic tradecraft, sufficient resources, and patience. This generational challenge cannot be limited by a four-year presidential term, nor can it produce instant solutions that would fit nicely in a Pentagon PowerPoint presentation. Even if we have clear metrics to measure the progress of the public diplomacy effort, such progress will be slow, incremental, and frequently difficult to quantify.

The WMD Commission called on the intelligence community to maximize its support for public diplomacy through enhanced expertise on other cultures and societies. Such expertise must be nuanced and sophisticated. In chapter 8 of its 2005 report, the WMD Commission warned that knowing the context of political Islam and Islamic activism is critical to effective public diplomacy: "Many of the intelligence challenges of today and tomorrow will . . . be transnational and driven by non-state actors. Analysts who cover these issues will need to know far more than the inclinations of a handful of senior government officials; they will need a deep understanding of the trends and shifts in local political views, cultural norms, and economic demands. For example, analysts seeking to identify geographic areas likely to be receptive to messages of violence toward the United States will need to be able to distinguish such areas from those that, while espousing anti-U.S. rhetoric or advancing policies at odds with the interests of the United States, nevertheless eschew violent tactics." The commission's report concluded by saying, "Failure to think creatively about how to develop an analytic cadre with a deep understanding of cultures very different from our own will seriously undermine the Community's ability to respond to the new and different challenges of the 21st century." Reaching out to other cultures, or what the State Department calls cultural diplomacy, is at the heart of a successful public diplomacy. According to a 2005 State Department report, "Cultural diplomacy is the linchpin of public diplomacy; for it is in cultural activities that a nation's idea of itself is best represented. And cultural diplomacy can enhance our national security in subtle, wide-ranging, and sustainable ways. . . . In the wake of the invasion of Iraq, the prisoner abuse scandal at Abu Ghraib, and the controversy over the handling of detainees at Bagram (Afghanistan) and Guantanamo Bay, America is viewed in much of the world less as a beacon of hope than as a dangerous force to be countered."

CAVEATS AND CHALLENGES

Public diplomacy must be distinguished from other overt and covert government initiatives targeting Islamic terrorism. In the years following 9/11, policymakers talked about three components of public diplomacy: promote universal values of democracy, especially the rule of law and good governance; discredit the radical ideology; and empower Islamic moderates in different Muslim countries. It is easy to see how these three objectives can have contradictory unintended outcomes. For example, how much should American public diplomacy push for universal values of civil rights and good governance (accountability, transparency, rule of law, freedom of political choice and assembly, etc.) when many of the regimes the United States cooperates with on the counterterrorism front are authoritarian and not ready to relinquish control anytime soon? If freedom of speech is one of those universal values, how should the administration react to the harassment and silencing of pro-democracy liberal dissidents? And how will such reaction be interpreted by ruling elites, pro-democracy oppositionists, and average Muslims? If public diplomacy pushes for free and fair elections as a tangible symbol of democracy, as was the case in the Palestinian territories, will the U.S. government be prepared to live with the results? American rejection of the Hamas election cast a long shadow on Washington's credibility as a spokesman for universal democratic values.

Promoting "moderation" can be another precarious and challenging goal for American public diplomacy makers who have to be extremely careful in raising questions about the so-called Islamic reformation and moderate Islam. How do they in fact define a "moderate" Muslim? Is it by the degree of piety, the person's stand on terrorism, or whether that person is critical or supportive of U.S. foreign policy? As the WMD Commission said, what metrics does the U.S. government have in assessing a Muslim's "moderation" when that person opposes terrorism but at the same time opposes American policy on other issues pertaining to the Islamic world? Perhaps the public diplomacy paradigm should excise the words "moderate" and "moderation" from its lexicon and replace them with "tolerant" and "tolerance." Excising other phrases such as "global war on terror" and "if we don't fight them there, they will follow us here" from our public utterances is equally important in designing an imaginative public policy paradigm. To counter the possibility that Muslims believe that the "war on terror" is a war on Islam, it is only logical that policymakers banish "war" from fighting terrorism and pursue terrorist criminals with vigor. If empowering "tolerant" Muslims is the right strategy, how can it be accomplished without involving indigenous credible Muslim voices? It will be a major challenge to identify these voices that have credibility in their communities and beyond and have the ability to write or speak in local languages. Of course, it remains to be seen whether these indigenous advocates of tolerance have the physical and moral courage to tell radical Wahhabis and other Sunni and Shia extremists that violence and terrorism are inimical to Islam and that a strict, narrow-minded interpretation of seventh-century Muslim texts does not serve the interests of Islam in the twenty-first century.

SECULARISTS AND MODERNISTS

American policymakers would do well to remember that Muslim audiences generally can be divided into three categories: secularists, modernists or reformists, and strict traditionalists. Secular Muslims are those who advocate separating religion from politics and public policy and who tend to relegate religion to the private realm, although they support having Islamic law (*Sharia*) govern personal status law, such as marriage, divorce, and inheritance. They might be personally pious but do not agree with the traditional Muslim Brotherhood teaching that Islam is a total way of life or that Islam is the solution to society's ills. Secularists are usually professionals or business people, are relatively more educated than the average citizen, are members of the middle or upper-middle class, and tend to send their children to the best schools (including private Christian schools). For example, most students at a Catholic K–12 school for girls in the West Bank are Muslims. Other Catholic schools in Jordan, Lebanon, Syria, Egypt, Kuwait, United Arab Emirates, and Tunisia similarly have large enrollments of Muslim students. Politically, secular Muslims follow national and international news on satellite television stations and through national and regional newspapers and magazines. They might be critical of American foreign policy regarding specific issues or conflicts such as Palestine, Lebanon, Syria, Iran, and Iraq, but they do not support global Islamic jihad, terrorism, or al-Qaʿida. Many of them practice their religion, participate in religious rituals, and rely on their faith as a moral compass for their personal behavior and family relations but do not bring religion into the public sphere unless it pertains to a specific local or national issue. Nor are they well versed in religion and Qurʾanic studies. Where there are national elections, secularists tend to vote for an Islamic party because of its perceived honesty, credibility, and service to the community; in many cases, voting for such a party is a protest vote against perceived corrupt and repressive policies of the leadership in power.

Muslim secularists often find themselves in a bifurcated state of mind about the role of religion in society. While they support relegating religion to the private sphere, they are reticent to express their views publicly lest they be accused by the regime of spreading *fitna* or discord or being branded by extremists as anti-Islam or apostates. Unlike in Western countries where separation of church and state is enshrined in national constitutions, most Arab states, where secular Muslims live, recognize Islam as the official religion of the states and *Sharia* as "the" or "a" source of legislation. Secularists are small in number, lack a strong political base, and are usually marginalized by regimes and viewed with suspicion because of their support of human rights, freedom of speech and assembly, government accountability and transparency, and limiting the powers of the executive. Secularists are often receptive to American public diplomacy and can find common ground with Western Christian nations.

The modernists or reformists tend to be more active in political Islam, are familiar with the traditions of the faith, and are comfortable with the history of reform and reformist thinkers in recent centuries in Islam. Constituting the majority of Muslims worldwide, they seek to reinterpret Islam to suit a twenty-first-century globalized world. They argue that the Qur'an, revealed to the Prophet Muhammad in seventh-century Arabia, must be universalized in the context of Islamic and world realities fourteen centuries later now that the vast majority of Muslims are not Arabs and do not live in the Arab heartland of Islam. Furthermore, the classical geographic separation between the abode of Islam or *dar al-Islam* where most Muslims lived and the abode of war or the *dar al-harb* where non-Muslims lived has become blurred. The Ottoman Empire, which encompassed the world of Islam and the Islamic Caliphate, disappeared, and tens of millions of Muslims today live in non-Muslim countries, under non-Muslim rule, and are equal citizens of Christian, Hindu, or Jewish polities. In fact, much of the modernizing debate today occurs in Christian countries, especially

Western Europe and the United States, where Muslims are a minority but where they enjoy full citizenship and practice the freedom of speech, thought, and worship.

The central argument of reformist thinkers is that traditional Islamic teachings and institutions are not incompatible with modern institutions of government and such concepts as *shura* or consultation and *ijma'* or consensus can easily be translated into modern concepts of democracy. Furthermore, reformist thinkers employ modern scientific and technological methods, especially in business and communications, to manage regional and global corporations; they maintain that Islamic finance, for example, can be a major player in the global economy and do not hesitate to use electronic connectivity and modern business and management practices to further their goal of economic prosperity. The author has met dozens of reformists in several Muslim countries who are active participants in the debate on the role of Islam in the modern world that is currently raging among Muslims. Much of this debate—most of which has not been translated into English or, if it is in English, has not been translated into Arabic—can be followed in newspaper columns, on television talk shows, at book fairs and literary gatherings, in academic institutions, and at regional and international scholarly conferences. The bottom line of the reformist argument is that Islam must interact with other cultures and civilizations and could benefit from modern ideas, scientific thinking and innovation imported from outside the Islamic world. The scientific method should be employed to encourage freethinking by Muslims about all kinds of subjects, including religion, without fear of retribution from the self-appointed guardians of the faith.

Reformist thinking aims at liberating the believer from the stifling environment of doctrinal uniformity and imposed consensus. Like the secularists, many Muslim reformists, as public opinion polls and the author's interviews have shown, can be extremely critical of American foreign policy, especially of America's "war on terror" and of the Bush doctrine regarding the use of American military power around the world. But they support the values of tolerance and good governance and reject the radical ideology and terrorism. Modernizing thinking, at the theological level, represents the critical mass of mainstream Islam and should be the target of a creative American public diplomacy. Unlike the secularists, Islamic reformists and modernists do not believe in a separation of church and state and view Islam as a total way of life encompassing faith, society, and politics.

In this regard, these thinkers reject the whole concept of secularism as contradictory to Islam; they are even more adamant in their rejection of the Kemalist "laicism" doctrine in Turkey, which bans the role of religion in society altogether. In an Arabic-language article titled "The Muslim Brotherhood and Cotemporary Islamic Parties" (ikhwanonline.com, August 5, 2007), Muhammad Marsi, a Muslim Brotherhood thinker and a member of its Guidance Bureau (*maktab al-irshad*), offered a thoughtful but critical analysis of the stand of Arab Islamic political parties on the electoral victory of AKP in the Turkish parliamentary elections. While he congratulated AKP on its success, he said the MB cannot possibly emulate the AKP political program because of AKP's support for secularism. He said the MB and other Arab Islamic political parties advocate a centrist political ideology grounded in Islam. These parties do not view secular ideology as the hallmark of governance, which the AKP endorses, because Arab societies are highly Islamized and Islamic law and traditions permeate the entire society. The goal of AKP is a secular state, but "our greatest fundamental goal is for Muslims to have an Islamic State [*dawla Islamiyya*; the author used the English translation in the article] and not a religious state as it is erroneously understood in the West. . . . Unlike AKP, which represents Turkey's secular tradition and which is working relentlessly to bring Turkey into the European fold, the MB's constitution states that Islam is the official religion of the state and *Sharia* is the source of legislation." It is interesting to note that Prime Minister Recep Tayyib Erdogan, the head of AKP, has been promoting "secularism" (separation of church and state) in his speeches since the reelection of AKP and downplaying the Kemalist concept of "laicism" (banning of religion from public life). The Muslim Brotherhood rejects both as inimical to true Islam, arguing that basing a political party's ideology, as AKP has done, on an Islamic foundation while defending secularism does not reflect a genuine commitment to Islam. If approached carefully and with sensitivity, reformist Islam can be a fertile ground for a new cultural and public diplomacy. Although U.S. policymakers should welcome the energized reformist debate within Islam, they should not get involved in the debate itself, which should be left to credible Muslim thinkers and scholars. It is difficult for a non-Muslim to participate in the "modernizing" or *tajdid* (renewal) debate; having sat in numerous gatherings with Islamic activists discussing these issues, I realized that even Islamic activists, many of whom are steeped in Islamic studies, disagreed on the meaning of these concepts. The theological debates within Islam, as in Christianity and Judaism, have been going on for centuries, and Islamic reformist thought has advanced significantly in the past two centuries. The writings and discourse of nineteenth- and twentieth-century reformists and *tajdidis* or "renewalists" such as Khayr al-Din al-Tunisi (1810–90), Rifaʿat al-Tahtawi (1801–73), Abd al-Rahman al-Kawakibi (1854–1902), Jamal al-Din al-Afghani (1838–97), Muhammad Abdu (1849–1905), Rashid Rida (1865–1935), Qasim Amin (1863–1908), Ali Abd al-Raziq (1888–1966), and Taha Hussein (1889–1973) have spread throughout the Islamic world and left a lasting impact on Islamic political thought and the relationship between Islam and non-Islamic cultures. Contemporary reformist thinkers such as Abd al-Karim Soroush (Iran), Mohsen Kadivar (Iran), Shaykh Muhammad Hussein Fadlallah (Lebanon), Shaykh Ahmad Kuftaru (Syria), Muhammad Shahrur (Syria), Muhammad Arkun (France and Algeria), Hasan Hanafi (Egypt), Khalid Abu el-Fadl (United States), Abdullahi Ahmad al-Naʿim (United States and Sudan), Farish Noor (Malaysia), Fahmy Huwaydi (Egypt), Asghar Ali Engineer (India), and Tariq Ramadan (Switzerland) are continuing the tradition of earlier *tajdidis* through their effort to adapt the Islam of seventh-century Arabia to a multicultural world characterized by globalization and pluralism.

The term "moderate" in this context means that these intellectuals publicly oppose global terrorism, reject the rigid interpretation of Islam advocated by Usama Bin Ladin and other al-Qa'ida leaders, and generally support the introduction of modern concepts such as democracy into Islamic thinking. They further maintain that the key components of Western theories of government—for example, parliamentary democracy, political pluralism, women's rights, and human rights in general—are compatible with Islamic texts and traditions. They seek a comfortable ground between Western values and Islamic legitimacy, and many argue that generalized political and cultural reform must go hand in hand with theological reform in the Islamic world. It would be naive and counterproductive for a non-Muslim interested in influencing these developments to think that Islamic "reformation" is around the corner, and all that is missing is a "Muslim Martin Luther." Despite this rich intellectual tradition, Islam remains under the control of traditional Sunni 'ulama and Shia grand ayatollahs, and Muslim states for the most part have not allowed open and free reformist debates on the future of Islam and its renewal. The challenge to American public diplomacy is that reformist mainstream Islam, which should be the focus of the United States, is also the target of radical jihadists. Therefore, countering the radical message should be at the center of U.S. public diplomacy.

TRADITIONALISTS AND RADICAL SALAFIS

Strict traditionalists, or the so-called fundamentalists or Salafis, are the most difficult target for American public diplomacy, and some of them are not at all receptive to American overtures or explanations about American foreign policy. Traditionalists, primarily Sunni Muslims, might be divided into three groups: those who read the Qur'an and the Hadith (Muhammad's sayings) literally and who espouse a narrow interpretation of their religion and an exclusivist vision, believe Islam is the only route to salvation, but do not participate in violence or terrorism; those who hold the same narrow interpretation of Islam but view violent jihad as an acceptable means for political change and for bringing about a global Islamic state or a caliphate; and those who support terrorism and engage in it against the "ene-mies" of Islam. All three groups, who call themselves Salafis or neo-Salafis but who are called Wahhabis by others, adhere to the teachings of Ahmad ibn Hanbal (who founded the Hanbali School of jurisprudence in Sunni Islam in the ninth century) and Muhammad ibn Abd al-Wahhab (who lived in the Arabian Peninsula in the eighteenth century and is the father of Wah-habis). They hold a purist view of Islam and advocate a return to the *salaf* or the early ancestors of Islam—namely, the Prophet and the first four "rightly guided" caliphs or successors to Mu-hammad. Their understanding of the Muslim doctrine is strictly based on the Qur'an, the Hadith, and the *Sunna* or traditions of the *salaf* or ancestors. They shun the "infidels" (even though Christians and Jews are described in the Qur'an as the "People of the Book"), encourage their followers not to interact with them, and believe that these "infidels" (including citizens of the United States and its allies, Israelis, and pro-American Arab and Muslim leaders) have waged a war on Islam and are therefore the "far" and "near"enemy of Islam. It is the duty of all Muslims to do jihad against this enemy. Their millenarian violent strug-gle for the soul and continued survival of Islam will continue until the "end of days" when Islam will emerge victorious. They are equally intolerant of "secular" or "modernist" Muslims and do not hesitate to brand their co-religionists *kuffar* (plural of *kafir*, meaning unbelievers) or apostates, which thereby justifies killing them.

The first group tends to read the scriptures literally without any deviation and believes that Islam was revealed by God in its entirety as a complete corpus of faith and cannot be changed. In a sense, they are not much different from "fundamentalist" Christians and Jews who read their holy scriptures literally. They shun other religions and their followers but do not engage in or support violent jihad. They tend to pursue their ultimate goal of establishing an Islamic state through peaceful means. They are not friendly to the West and have been very critical of American policy toward the Muslim world and of American values, which they consider permissive, promiscuous, and a threat to Islamic family values. They reject Western-style democracy, which calls for popular sovereignty, as an intrusion from the outside and a violation of God's rule on earth. They maintain that Islam, which already has its own democracy, divinely prescribed, through the practice of *bay'a* (the community's allegiance to the ruler), *shura* (consultation), and *ijma'* (consensus), must not follow Western "man-made" democracy. Although reaching out to this group is extremely challenging, it might be possible for U.S. public diplomacy officials to engage some of the thinkers in this group on a selective basis, focusing on the common themes between Islamic democracy and Western theories of representative government.

The second group of radical Islamic activists, although very similar to the first group in ideology and attitude toward non-Muslims, differs on the nature of jihad. Although they think it is possible to work for an Islamic state peacefully, there are situations and conditions—such as pervasive regime repression or collaboration between Muslim regimes and "infidels" against the perceived interests of Islam—that might legitimize the use of violence to remove a regime or to change the political system of a particular country. When a Muslim territory is under attack or occupation, or when the Sunni community is being oppressed, Muslims should use all means to liberate it and to end the oppression of Sunnis, including suicide bombings and acts of terror. This position, they argue, is not a blank endorsement of terrorism and suicide bombings that result in the killing of innocent civilians; it applies only to specific situations such as the Palestinian territories, Iraq, Kashmir, and Chechnya. Their support of violent jihad is selective, depending on situations where Muslims find themselves under duress and where violence is the only available option. A radical proponent of this position told me on a visit to a Muslim country, "If we have the same military capability as the aggressor, we would use it; otherwise, we have to use the weapon of the weak, which in this case means suicide bombings." Members of this group also view the West as the enemy of Islam, intent on humiliating Muslims and keeping Islamic countries weak, and they perceive Western anti-Islamic policies as racist and bigoted. Although traditionalist in religious outlook and rabidly anti-Western and anti-

Christian, these clerics do not hesitate to use Western technology to spread their message on the Internet through *fatwas*, commentaries, and analysis; some of them even have their own blogs. Among the most prominent names in this group are Salman al-Awda (Saudi), Yusif al-Qaradawi (Egyptian by birth but lives in Qatar), Safar al-Hawali (Saudi), Harith Sulayman al-Dhari (Iraqi), and Majdi Ahmad Hussein (Egyptian). Members of this group would be less receptive than the first group of traditionalists to American public diplomacy initiatives and to contacts with Americans, but, according to press reports, some of the thinkers in the group, for example, Yusif al-Qaradawi, would be willing to engage American public policy officials on issues of good governance. If there is a genuine movement on the peace front between Israel and the Palestinians, al-Qaradawi could become an occasional interlocutor with American diplomats against extremism.

The third group is the most radical and the most supportive of violent jihad and terrorism. American public diplomacy should not spend any effort or resources trying to reach this group, but American policymakers should be aware of the group's enormous capability in recruiting jihadists and terrorists. Members of this group are convinced that Islam is engaged in an existential struggle with its enemies and that violent jihad is the only recourse available to Muslims if they hope to win this struggle. The killing of innocent civilians can be justified, as Bin Ladin has argued since the late 1990s, in the larger battle against the infidels either because of their presence near the battlefield or because of their indirect culpability, especially in a democracy where they elect leaders who wage war against Islam. They justify terrorism, especially spreading fear in the ranks of the enemy, as an effective and legitimate tool in their fight on behalf of Islam. Radical Islamic activists usually seek guidance for their jihad, or for specific jihadist operations, from radical clerics or religious scholars, many of whom are graduates of the Islamic University in Medina, Um al-Qura in Mecca, and Imam Muhammad in Riyadh and often live in Saudi Arabia or other Gulf Arab states. These clerics, known as *fuqaha' al-jihad* (scholars of jihad), tend to be Salafi or Wahhabi; they are followers of Sayyid

Qutb, who represented the radical extreme of the Muslim Brotherhood, and adherents of a thirteenth–fourteenth century religious scholar by the name of Ibn Taymiyya (1263–1328). They believe in the Wahhabi *tawhidi* (oneness of God and the universe) doctrine and the practice of *takfir* (declaring other Muslims unbelievers). Sayyid Qutb described Muslim leaders who do not follow the dictates of Islam in their governance as living in a state of *jahiliyya* (ignorance of the true faith) and should be removed from power by all means, including by force.

Jihadist clerics also believe that Islam will not regain its stature unless the caliphate is reestablished. (In fact, Bin Ladin, who frequently quotes some of these clerics, has lamented the elimination of the Muslim Caliphate by Mustafa Kemal Ataturk after World War I and has called for its restoration.) They also view ongoing conflicts in parts of the Muslim world (Palestine, Chechnya, Kashmir, Indonesia, etc.) not as discrete conflicts but as part of the infidels' global war on Islam, which Muslims worldwide must repel. To them, the continued control of Jerusalem by the "Jews" is particularly offensive because of the city's sacred place in Islam. They do not recognize Israel and view it as a symbol of "Jewish" usurpation of Muslim lands and are critical of any party, including the Palestinian Authority, that would negotiate with the "Jews" over the fate of an Islamic trust. They accuse the "Jews" of "conniving" and "deceit" and compare them to the "Jews" of seventh-century Arabia, who "reneged" on their treaty with Muhammad and "conspired" against him. Muslims, these clerics argue, should take a lesson from the Battle of Badr in 624 in which Muhammad's armies defeated the "polytheists and the Jews" and plan for removing today's Jews from Palestine. Radical clerics do not place much emphasis on the Qur'anic teachings that Jews and Christians are "People of the Book" and describe them as enemies of Islam; they teach instead, relying on a questionable Hadith, that Christianity and Judaism shall not be allowed to exist in Saudi Arabia, the "Land of the Two Holy Shrines" (Mecca and Medina). They do not consider the Shia as true Muslims but as rejectionists (*rafida*) of Islam and collaborators with the enemies of Islam, who must be decimated. This is the reason why these clerics support the insurgency in Iraq, especially its anti-Shia focus, and encourage Saudi and other young men to go to Iraq and do jihad against the American occupation and the Shia.

Several radical clerics have been frequently arrested in Saudi Arabia for their views and moral and financial support of violent jihad and al-Qaʿida; some of them have "recanted" their previous statements and abandoned their radical ideology, according to the Saudi government. Among the most well-known radical scholars of this group are Hamid al-Ali (Kuwaiti), Nasir al-Umar (Saudi), Nasir al-Fahd (Saudi), Sulayman Abu al-Ghayth (Kuwaiti), Ali al-Khudayr (Saudi), Abu Muhammad al-Maqdisi (Palestinian), Hammud bin Uqla al-Shuʿaybi (Saudi), Sulayman bin Nasir al-Ulaywan (Saudi), and Abd al-Rahman bin Nasir al-Barrak (Saudi). These scholars and clerics can be described as "enablers" of violent jihad and terrorism in that they provide a religious justification for terror. They usually provide their guidance through mosque sermons, schools and religious institutes, and the electronic and print media, including cassettes. Although this group will not under any circumstances respond positively to American public diplomacy, American policymakers should pay serious attention to it because of the large influence its prominent clerics exert on some segments of Muslim youth. They recruit the same youths and Islamic activists that future American public diplomacy must hope to engage, and they lump ideology and policy together, which makes it easier for them to recruit activists who are critical of American policy. A key challenge of U.S. public diplomacy is to decouple the two and work diligently to undercut Salafi ideology and explain U.S. policy.

The United States public diplomacy faces two additional serious challenges: first, the tension between "selling" public diplomacy to the Muslim world in the context of specific foreign policies toward specific Muslim countries and regions; and, second, understanding Muslim expectations and likely receptivity to public diplomacy. The first challenge revolves around how to explain public diplomacy, for example, to the Middle East, while the U.S. occupation remains in Iraq and Afghanistan, the Israeli occupation of the West Bank continues, and undemocratic re-

gimes are still in power. Selling policy, of course, would be much
easier if the U.S. occupation ended; if not, it will be much harder
to persuade Muslims of the seriousness of American efforts to
engage them. Despite continued Israeli occupation, however,
public diplomacy could promote "bread and butter" issues that
are of primary concern to the average Palestinian. These include
the ability of Palestinian farmers to reach their fields without
harassment, providing job opportunities for Palestinian youth
within the territories and inside Israel, ending the daily humiliation at military and security checkpoints, slowly dismantling
the occupation, providing adequate educational opportunities
to Palestinian youth, and easing travel between West Bank and
Gaza towns and cities. As the conflict between Israel and the
Palestinians remains unresolved, public diplomacy should promote reasonable expectations for the Palestinians, which for a
Palestinian young man translates into finding a job, saving
money, getting married, and building a home. Such expectations will begin to generate hope instead of hopelessness and
real progress instead of victimization and defeatism. An employed young man with a wife and a home generally does not
respond readily to recruitment by radicals and terrorists. Of
course, exceptions abound, but many of the jihadist "foot soldiers" have a limited education and are unemployed, single,
alienated males with very little hope for the future. Although
the United States has been unable to solve the Israeli-Palestinian
conflict, its pursuit of dialogue and continuous efforts to bring
the parties together—from the late 1970s to the late 1990s—
were praised by Arabs and Muslims for their fairness and balance. U.S. public diplomacy should endeavor to recapture that
image.

According to academic experts, the tension between policy
and diplomacy will undermine the success of public diplomacy
as long as the policy on Iraq, Afghanistan, and Guantanamo has
not changed, because it will be extremely challenging to defend
international norms, the rule of law, and rights of innocent civilians if the United States continues to hold detainees in Guantanamo and other detention centers in Iraq, Afghanistan, and
elsewhere without indictments or trials. These experts maintain

that unless the "global war on terror" is recast, and unless Muslims are convinced that it is not a war against Islam but against criminals, public diplomacy will not succeed in spreading its rule-of-law message. The other challenge facing public diplomacy is the question of democracy, political reform, and free elections. The United States' support of these objectives, which lie at the heart of the American political value system, can succeed only if American policy is committed—in word and in deed—to working with governments and civil society institutions to effect democratization and political reform. Arab pro-democracy advocates have argued that if the United States refuses to accept the results of free national elections because the winner is opposed to American policy, public diplomacy will find itself in an untenable situation. The other part of the democracy equation is the United States' continued close relationship with authoritarian regimes because they serve America's other global interests—namely, the fight against terrorism. Human rights advocates have also argued that United States' financial and military aid to these regimes and its refusal to engage pro-democracy civil society activists in a meaningful manner casts doubt on America's sincerity in defense of democracy. The United States' positive response to demands for democracy and political reform, which cut across different segments of Muslim societies, can be a strong weapon in the arsenal of American public diplomacy.

My discussions with Arab and Muslim interlocutors in the past dozen years, reveal that their expectations for U.S. public diplomacy are clear on some issues and muddled on others, which makes it more challenging for policymakers. According to public opinion polls, Arabs and Muslims are very clear on what they expect of the United States: fairness, justice, and a balanced and evenhanded approach to international conflicts. A Muslim university professor told me in an interview, "As the United States has the oldest functioning democracy in the world, we expect it to stand up for the rule of law, for open and transparent government, and against repression and corruption without equivocation." American public diplomacy should help guarantee the voters' right to cast their ballot freely, without harassment or manipulation by the regime; it can engage on this issue easily if the underlying policy of the United States is genuinely supportive of democratic change and political reform.

On other issues, Islamic activists' expectations of American foreign and public diplomacy seem to lack clarity. Reformers, for example, are not sure what they want the United States to do with their regimes. Some argue that American foreign policy should be critical of authoritarian regimes' record of human rights abuse and their refusal to open up the political system, yet these same activists would strongly object to outside interference, especially through the use of the military, that might lead to regime change. They demand good governance based on transparency, accountability, and the rule of law but are unclear how to achieve it. For many reformers, despite their struggle for political reform and the regime's persistent refusal to democratize, national sovereignty always prevails over foreign-induced regime change. When one of them was asked if he really wanted the United Stated to intervene, he replied, "Maybe yes, maybe no, I really don't know!" On the issue of terrorism, modernist thinkers have skirted the issue and shied away from offering a nonradical interpretation of violent jihad; although many of them condemned the September 11, 2001 attacks, they have avoided getting involved in public theological debates on the Qur'an and violence. Nor have Muslim regimes encouraged such a public debate. Islamic activists' clouded vision on some of these issues makes it more challenging for the United States to draw up a clear public diplomacy program but, on the other hand, operating in an environment of tolerable ambiguity might allow policymakers to be even more creative in their approach to diverse Muslim audiences.

CORE THEMES

President Bush's appointment of a special envoy to the Organization of the Islamic Conference (OIC) on March 5, 2008, is an indication of the U.S. government's serious interest in reaching out to Muslims. Such an ambassador, both now and in the future, needs to have a clear understanding of the American and Muslim contexts in which he is operating. In addition, he must familiarize himself with the core issues of concern to the Islamic world. Before he embarks on any mission, he must be sure to synchronize his message with specific policies. For example, if he announces a "new" public diplomacy initiative on the Palestinian conflict, it would have to reflect a genuine substantive policy change on the issue as well. Otherwise, American officials will be accused, as they have been in the past, of sending mixed messages, resulting in failure. The core themes that might make a strong headway with Muslim audiences will be those that focus on commonalities rather than differences between religions. Specific policies that produce immediate and tangible results in localized communities can also be effective tools of communication. The envoy should also know that targeting terrorists and terrorism is a short-term challenge, but understanding and deciphering the societal context of diverse Muslim societies in which terrorists and radicals operate are long-term challenges requiring, among other things, endless patience. An envoy would do well to have a threefold strategic focus: undermine and marginalize the radical paradigm; encourage progressive, tolerant Islam (or what the Malaysian prime minister called "Islam Hadhari"); and promote universal values of good governance, including representative government, freedom of expression, and human rights.

The core themes of public diplomacy should revolve around a single narrative, with which mainstream Muslims can identify and to which they would positively respond. In order to succeed, however, public diplomacy must be coupled with a new American foreign policy committed to resolving the Israeli-Palestinian conflict, ending the conflict in Iraq, and pushing for economic and political reform in the region. The following ten core themes stand out:

1. The United States is not engaged in a conflict with Islam; on the contrary, the international community is fighting terrorists who in the name of Islam bring untold suffering on inno-

cent Muslims and non-Muslims alike. Terrorism and the killing of innocent civilians affect us all, regardless of race, color, religion, or geography.

2. Islam, Christianity, and Judaism share many noble ideas, including justice, fairness, compassion, love of family, the sanctity of life, and the right to make choices freely. They abhor the targeting and killing of innocent civilians.

3. People of all faiths aspire for dignity, respect, equality, education, economic opportunity, progress, and security.

4. People should be able to select their government freely, and that government should be transparent, accountable, and just. It should be committed to the rule of law; freedom of thought, speech, and association; and respect for all citizens, including minorities.

5. The United States is committed to actively engage Muslim communities and to help foster debate about a peaceful and creative future vision of Islam. However, Muslims should be the primary participants in this debate; the United States does not intend to drive the debate.

6. Most Muslims are choosing freedom and progress over the violence and tyranny that violent extremists advocate. The United States and most of the Muslim world are on the side of freedom and progress.

7. The United States is committed to a definition of terrorism that is acceptable to the international community and will work with Muslim scholars to devise the most appropriate and culturally sensitive terminology regarding terrorism and the means to fight it. For example, American public diplomacy should avoid the use of such al-Qaʿida terms as "jihad" and "caliphate," and replace them with the Arabic word *hiraba* (crimes against society). "Hunt for terrorist criminals" and similar phrases should be substituted for the heretofore provocative "global war on terror."

8. The United States is committed to work with Muslim leaders and communities to settle regional disputes on the basis of justice, fairness, and equity in accordance with accepted international legal norms and conventions and United Nations resolutions.

9. American public diplomacy is committed to partner with indigenous, credible Muslim activists and groups for political reform and economic and educational opportunity. These include mainstream Islamic political parties; civil society organizations and professional associations; grade school and high school teachers; print and electronic journalists, editorialists, and commentators; reformist Islamic thinkers and clerics, especially younger clerics working at community and neighborhood mosques and religious centers; and women's organizations in smaller communities that focus on social, health, and employment issues.

10. American public diplomacy is committed in the pursuit of its mission to involve the American Muslim community's activist organizations, which could play a constructive role in designing the message to Muslim audiences, communicating with other Muslims, and advancing the cause of tolerance, pluralism, and progressive Islam.

Mainstream Muslims would respond positively to a redefinition of the terminology and tools to combat terrorism because of their strong condemnation of the terrorist attacks on 9/11. For example, on September 14, 2001, leaders of several Islamic political parties and movements plus forty other religious scholars issued the following statement: "The undersigned, leaders of Islamic movements, are horrified by the events of Tuesday 11 September 2001 in the United States which resulted in massive killing, destruction and attack on innocent lives. . . . We condemn, in the strongest terms, the incidents, which are against all human and Islamic norms. This is grounded in the Noble Laws of Islam which forbid all forms of attacks on civilians." The statement was signed by the heads of the Muslim Brotherhood (Egypt), Jama'at-i-Islam (Pakistan), Jama'at-i-Islam (Bangladesh), Islamic Resistance Movement (Hamas, Palestine), al-Nahda Renaissance Movement (Tunisia), Parti Islam SeMalaysia (Malaysia). Shaykh Yusif al-Qaradawi and a few other prominent scholars issued a *fatwa* on September 27, 2001, that said in part, "The terrorist acts, from the perspective of Islamic law, constitute the crime of *hiraba*." On September 15, 2001, the

Grand Mufti of Saudi Arabia also condemned the attacks by saying, "Hijacking planes, terrorizing innocent people and shedding blood constitute a form of injustice that cannot be tolerated by Islam, which views them as gross crimes and sinful acts." Muhammad Khatami, then president of Iran, on November 9, 2001, issued the following statement: "The horrific terrorist attacks of September 11, 2001, in the United States were perpetrated by a cult of fanatics who had self-mutilated their ears and tongues, and could communicate with perceived opponents only through carnage and devastation." If American public diplomacy can recapture the antiterrorism feelings that swept the world right after 9/11, the United States should be in a position to segregate the terrorists from the majority of Muslims and marginalize them.

State-supported terrorism poses a different kind of challenge because of the murkiness of the linkage between the government and other official organs of the state and terrorist groups and organizations and the difficulty counterterrorism analysis usually encounters in tracking and deciphering such linkages. Iran is a case in point: open-source information about Iran's perceived support of Shia and Sunni militias and terrorist groups in Iraq encompasses moral encouragement, strategizing, funding, training, and in some cases weapons, but it offers no clear evidence regarding the magnitude and nature of such support. Two questions arise: First, is the Iranian military support limited to a specific situation, for example, arming the Iraqi insurgency against the occupation (which many Sunni and Shia Muslims do not perceive as terrorism), or is it global through al-Qaʿida and other radical groups? Second, is such support given by an official organ of the government or by individuals or organizations that are either loosely connected to the government or only tolerated by the government?

Iran's response to an American initiative would signal the sincerity of its commitment to fighting terrorism. From the mid-1950s to the late 1970s, the United States considered Iran the cornerstone of Persian Gulf security and worked closely with it to ensure regional stability. The Nixon Doctrine in 1969 looked to Iran to play a pivotal role in the security of the region "east of Suez" because Iran was an oil country and the largest, most populated, and most powerful regional state; it was also led by a pro-Western regime. Iran's geostrategic position during the Cold War was of immense interest to the United States: it had the longest shore line of any riparian state on the Persian Gulf; it bordered on Pakistan and Afghanistan in the east, Iraq in the west, and the former Soviet Union in the north; and it had close relations with its Arab neighbors across the Gulf and with Israel. Despite the end of the Cold War and the change of regime in Tehran, Iran remains a major player in the Persian Gulf region with regional geopolitical interests and ambitions. Iran might argue that its perceived pro-terrorism activities are in fact no more than aiding "nationalist" Islamic groups that serve its national interest and geostrategic posture, which in the case of Iraq and Afghanistan would aim at the removal of American military presence from the eastern and western border regions of Iran. If that is the case, it might be possible to engage the Iranian leadership on geostrategic issues and explore compromises that could serve the long-term strategic interests of both countries. The key point here is that the United States should be able to engage Iran on mutually beneficial strategic issues, including the country's nuclear program, as long as regime change is not negotiable. Reaching out to Iran might resonate well in the Muslim world, even in Sunni states, because it would be viewed as a sign of American respect for a Muslim state's sovereignty and sensibilities. Two other advantages would accrue from a dialogue with Iran: it will help stabilize the sectarian violence and ethnic conflict in Iraq, and it would calm the anxieties of Gulf Arab states, including Saudi Arabia, about Iran's growing stature as a Shia state. A strategic engagement with Iran would also certainly strengthen American public diplomacy toward the Islamic world.

A Blueprint

In order to reach out to majorities of Muslims across the globe, the United States should devise a new public diplomacy encompassing a series of clear actions that would resonate with Muslims symbolically and tangibly. In order to convince Muslim publics and activists of the genuineness of America's intent, the proposed recommendations must go beyond rhetoric. Islamic activists and pro-democracy secular dissidents have heard enough speeches from American policymakers about how Islam is not the enemy, and how the United States is committed to democracy. As one activist told me, "Please, no more speeches!" Moreover, once recommendations are implemented, the public policy message should be conveyed by one messenger on behalf of the American president and government. The recommendations listed here are intended as a blueprint and are not new; in fact, they have appeared in several government and private public diplomacy commissions and reports since 9/11. Whenever a policymaker would ask why they were not implemented, my standard answer was, "I don't know; that's above my pay grade." The ten recommendations constitute a blueprint to guide future relations with the Islamic world.

Appoint an Ambassador to the Muslim World

The president's appointment of a special envoy to the Muslim world was a long-awaited response to calls by public diplomacy observers in recent years. Academic experts on Islam have suggested that the Muslim world would respond favorably to such an appointment because in Muslim minds the appointment would reflect a renewed American interest in Muslim affairs. Specifically, the Muslim world will expect the president's appointee to the OIC, which includes more than fifty-five Muslim states and territories, to be highly educated, well versed in Islamic issues, and fluent in Arabic or other "Islamic" languages. He would have high-level access to the White House as well as at the State Department. These qualifications would allow him to attend Islamic meetings wherever they are held, including in Mecca. He could visit Islamic universities and mosques all over the Islamic world and engage Muslim interlocutors—government officials and nongovernment organizations and groups—in substantive discussions and debates. He will be the only official American spokesman on Islamic issues and on United

States' political and diplomatic relations with the Muslim world and will work closely with American ambassadors to specific Muslim countries. Having an office in the White House is highly symbolic because it will signal to Muslim audiences that the new ambassador speaks for the president of the United States and is his principal adviser on Islamic affairs. He will also report to the secretary of state and act as the secretary's principal adviser on diplomatic and public policy relations with OIC member countries. The new ambassador will focus on regional Islamic issues, not bilateral relations between Muslim countries and the United States. The appointment of such an ambassador, not surprisingly, might ruffle some feathers at the State Department for bureaucratic reasons, but the underlying assumption of these recommendations is that the State Department will have already seen the need for a new and a more innovative public diplomacy and a more vigorous outreach program to the Muslim world. It should be emphasized that the appointment should be viewed as long term, not limited to the term of the president making the appointment. The appointee should be selected for his credentials on Islamic issues, not because of a special or financial relation with the president making the appointment.

Dialogue with Mainstream Islamic Political Parties

Building on the three-pronged premise that mainstream Islamic parties embody a reformist or centrist ideology, are committed to working within existing political systems, and are crucial to any genuine political reform and democratization, the United States must enter into a serious dialogue with these parties and establish a system of regular official contacts with them. Leaders of these parties—in Turkey, Jordan, Palestine, Lebanon, Egypt, Morocco, Kuwait, Bahrain, Malaysia, Pakistan, Bangladesh, and Indonesia—would welcome these contacts and would be eager to share their future vision of their societies and of Islam with American officials. Some of them would be critical of specific American policies, and it might be uncomfortable for U.S. officials to engage them, but it is imperative that the United States open up dialogue with these groups because oftentimes they are more credible representatives of their societies than the regimes in charge. As one moderate Islamic activist said, "Half the American people in the last presidential election voted for a different foreign policy, and majorities of Europeans disagree with your foreign policy. Doesn't the administration talk to them?" Furthermore, many of these parties have had a rich experience in local politics and elections and know firsthand the daily issues or *qadaya ma'ishiyya* (employment, education, health, poverty, hunger, etc.) that are of concern to their constituents. Their participation in the political process and in decision making (*al-musharaka fi sun' al-qarar*) through their membership in national legislatures positions them to understand the growing Islamization of Muslim societies and to direct their members and supporters away from violence and terrorism. Participation of these parties in the political process has contributed to their transformation and habituation and has forced them to engage with other blocs, regardless of their ideological differences, to pass legislation, and to compromise on projects that benefit their constituents and districts. These parties are above all indigenous entities and are not linked to any global radical or terrorist structure or organization.

Some of these groups, especially Hamas and Hizballah, are designated by the State Department as foreign terrorist organizations, which makes it difficult to initiate contacts with them. Perhaps it is time for the United States to follow the European model and take a more nuanced attitude toward Hizballah; the United States could designate some activities of Hamas and Hizballah as terrorist but not others. For example, the U.S. government could find common ground to work with either party on domestic governance issues, including government stability, political and financial reform, and civil society issues. At the same time, the U.S. government could take a much tougher stand on Hizballah's use of its media, such as the al-Manar satellite television station, and its intelligence apparatus to further an anti-American agenda and foment anti-American feelings. Both parties have developed extensive civil society systems of health, education, and welfare services to their communities without falling prey to corruption and nepotism. Hizballah, in particular, has collected donations from all over the world to fund many of its social welfare activities, and it is unwise in the long run to lump all these fundraising efforts and contributions under the rubric of terrorism. Admittedly, it is very difficult for analysts and experts to determine how many cents of how many dollars go to acceptable activities and to nefarious programs, but the lack of analytic precision should not automatically designate them terror-related funds. Engaging these parties would greatly enhance public diplomacy toward the Muslim world and open new doors among Islamic activists to American public policy officials.

Institutionalize American Commitment to Democracy

Foreign policy analysts and Arab and Muslim media reports have maintained that President Bush's call for democracy in his State of the Union speech in January 2005 failed to be translated into tangible policy because of the Iraq war, the need to cooperate with authoritarian rulers in the fight against terrorism, and the perception that the United States was trying to impose its brand of democracy on the world. Good governance, the rule of law, and civil rights should be placed at the center of U.S. foreign policy. Pro-democracy dissidents throughout the world have looked to the United States for moral—and some financial—support to further the cause of democracy and the right to challenge their autocratic and tyrannical rulers to no avail. They have heard uplifting rhetoric but saw little or no action. Autocrats remain ensconced in power with America's tacit support, the United States is bogged down in Iraq, and the cause of democracy is in retreat. The recommendation to dialogue with Islamic political parties should go hand in hand with the push for democracy and the rule of law. This recommendation does not advocate imposing American democratic ideals and values on the world, as some bureaucrats in Washington and authoritarian regimes have claimed; rather, it is a call on behalf of the universal right of people, as President Bush has stated, to reject tyranny and question their regimes' hold on power in perpetuity. Institutionalizing the commitment to democracy will entail reconfiguring the bureaucracy at the State Department and other appropriate agencies and departments and in the intelligence community to reflect new policies on behalf of democracy. The promotion of democracy, in word and in deed, can significantly strengthen the credibility of the United States. Democracy initiatives usually involve many people from different walks of life and levels of education and activism, whether in urban centers and rural areas, and focuses heavily on the civil society sector of the society. This recommendation, like the preceding one, will allow American public policy officials to interact with more diverse segments of society.

Develop a Parliamentarians' Exchange Program

In order to enhance dialogue with mainstream Islamic political parties, the United States could consider establishing a program under which Islamic party members in national legislatures are invited on three-month tours to visit state legislatures and the Congress of the United States. Visiting parliamentarians would shadow state legislators and individual members of Congress during the legislative session, both in the home districts and in Washington. Such a unique program would provide visiting Islamic parliamentarians a rare opportunity to witness the American legislative system in action and would give them a glimpse of how bills are proposed and passed and how compromises are made regardless of one's ideology. Members of Congress could in return visit some parliaments in selected Muslim countries. As more and more Islamic political parties and movements enter the political space through elections, through this program more rising Islamic politicians could be introduced to American representative and legislative processes on the state and national levels. The experience might be transforming for Muslim legislators and, through them, for their parties.

Expand Student, Faculty, and Professional Exchange Programs

Exchange programs for high school and college students, teachers, and university academics would entail a major funding increase to support travel, housing, and expenses of these students and faculty. Introducing Muslim students, faculty, journalists, judges, lawyers, and academics to American society and educational and other institutions and making them more aware of American values will in the long run enhance the country's counterterrorism efforts. Junior-senior high school exchange programs could be one-year long, with other programs ranging from three months to one year. Faculty research grants under the Fulbright and similar programs could be six to twelve months in length. Similar exchange programs could cover promising CEOs of smaller businesses, young business and management trainees and managers, and high school and college curriculum specialists. Under the education exchange program, the U.S. government in cooperation with American universities and state educational institutions could expand the sister university programs in which American universities would link up with their counterparts in Muslim countries leading to collaborative teaching and research, scientific experimentation, and conferences on a variety of subjects. American and Muslim professors could jointly teach specific courses on a rotating basis in the United States and in other countries. The sister university program could be emulated at the high school level. Because the educational level of a vast majority of Muslim youth does not exceed high school, it is urgent that American public diplomacy connects with high school students in those countries. The junior-senior year exchange program could be augmented with a national sister high school program that would bring high school teachers and administrators to visit, perhaps for three months, American middle and high schools in big cities as well in the heartland of America and introduce them to different pedagogical strategies and teaching techniques. The cumulative purpose of the academic exchange program would be to foster educational reform in some Islamic countries with an eye toward establishing a more inclusive and tolerant curriculum.

These programs will also require a comprehensive review of the visa policies of the United States with an eye toward facilitating the process of obtaining an entry visa to the United States. Between the early 1950s and the late 1990s, tens of thousands of

Arab and Muslim students studied in the United States in all kinds of subjects. Obtaining a student visa was relatively simple as long as an applicant received admission from an American college or university and had the financial means to pay for his or her education. Many returned to their home countries after receiving university degrees; others stayed and pursued successful careers in their field of study. Understandably, obtaining a visa after 9/11 has become very difficult for young single Arab or Muslim males, especially if the applicant is coming from a Middle Eastern or South Asian country. Once they entered the United States, visitors usually undergo questioning, finger printing, and other security measures, resulting in delays and, in some cases, personal humiliation. In reaction to the post-9/11 security environment, many potential applicants from Arab and Muslim countries have decided not to seek education in the United States or in the West in general and instead study at Middle Eastern universities. In recent years, however, other Western countries, especially Australia, Britain, and Canada, began to encourage potential Arab and other Middle Eastern students to study in their universities, giving these countries a windfall. In fact, students find the process of obtaining a visa to travel to those countries not cumbersome, the security procedures are not unduly inconvenient, and the tuition is much cheaper than in the United States. As a result, the United States is losing the opportunity to influence a whole generation of students and potential leaders.

Encourage American Universities to Build
Campuses in Muslim Countries

The experience of American education in the Middle East and elsewhere has been very positive. American colleges and universities in Lebanon, Turkey, and Egypt, especially the American University of Beirut (AUB) and the American University of Cairo (AUC), in the past hundred years, have graduated thousands of students, many of whom went on to assume leadership positions in their countries in government, commerce, and the professions. As part of my field research in Bahrain in the early

1970s, I traced the careers of Bahraini AUB graduates; I discovered that every one of them was a prosperous businessman, a medical doctor, a senior corporate manager, a literary figure, or a cabinet-level government appointee. American institutions of higher education in the Middle East have garnered the respect of host countries and offered high-quality education that has been the envy of the region. For example, during the violent, twenty-year civil war in Lebanon from the early 1970s to the late 1980s, warring factions assiduously avoided targeting the AUB campus despite the horrific destruction of the neighborhoods surrounding the university. The presidents of AUB, who have been American nationals, have been held in high esteem and protected by the community from harm with a few exceptions (unfortunately, one AUB president was assassinated during the civil war). Replicating this experiment will serve the long-term national interest of the United States because as generations of Arabs and Muslims are trained in a curriculum of modern education grounded in the scientific method of reason and discourse, they will help lead their societies away from violence and irrationality. American universities and foundations could either build satellite campuses in Arab and Muslim countries or open up new universities that would teach modern curricula that are certified by the American Association of Higher Education and similar certifying bodies, encompassing the sciences, liberal arts, business and management, technology, and the professions (especially medicine, dentistry, and public health). Of course, these universities will attract the elites who value education and can afford it, but with a creative academic scholarship and financial aid program, the student body could become more diverse, economically and socially.

Establish a National Imamate University

Working closely with appropriate universities and seminaries, the United States should push for the establishment of an imamate degree-granting institution of higher education in the United States. The mission of such an institution would be to train Muslim students in Islamic theology and jurisprudence and

Arabic language and at graduation grant them an advanced degree in Islamic theology and a certificate qualifying the graduating student to become an *imam* (a person who would lead people in prayer at the mosque) and a *mufti* (a person who would issue *fatwas* or religious edicts). An American imamate university would eliminate the need for foreign-trained imams or muftis to lead mosques and other places of Muslim prayer in the United States. Heretofore, imams at mosques in the United States were trained in Middle Eastern and South Asian Islamic universities and studied under a variety of Islamic curricula. Some of these universities, particularly in Saudi Arabia, offer a conservative Wahhabi curriculum, which inculcates students with a rigid interpretation of Islam. Many of today's radical clerics are graduates of these universities. In the United States, the American Association of Higher Education could form a committee comprising representatives from top universities and seminaries in the country to draw an appropriate curriculum for the proposed university. The committee would work closely with the Organization of the Islamic Conference and leading Islamic universities in the world, including al-Azhar in Egypt, the International Islamic University in Kuala Lumpur, and other universities in Morocco, Jordan, Lebanon, and Pakistan. It would also consult prominent Shia scholars at *hawzas* in Iraq and Iran and would work with large corporations and foundations to seek funding and an endowment for the university. This recommendation envisions the imamate university to become a center of Islamic theological studies in the United States and the Western world. The objective is to develop a curriculum that espouses moderate, tolerant, and inclusive interpretations of the Qur'an, the Hadith, and Islamic theology and jurisprudence. The university would open its doors to American and international students. Currently, the Hartford Seminary in Connecticut has the only licensed Muslim chaplaincy program in the country; however, the proposed imamate university would have a more comprehensive program of studies that could attract students from all over the Muslim world and could graduate generations of future clerics. The languages of instruction would be both English and Arabic.

Empower Muslim Reformers to Confront Radicalism

Reformist Muslim thinkers should be encouraged through indirect financial support to take on Islamic extremists on their own turf and in their languages. Nongovernmental research institutes, foundations, and think tanks should be established to help fund reformist thinkers' research, writing, and speaking about the dangers of extremism and the damage that terrorism has wrought on Muslim societies. If these reformists write in a foreign language, their writings should be translated, edited, and published in several Muslim countries in the local language—Arabic, Persian, Urdu, Dari, Pashtu, Malay, Bahasa Indonesia, or Swahili. The research institutes should also help program reformist intellectuals to appear on radio and television talk shows, especially al-Jazirah, and the Internet. In a similar vein, the research institutes should initiate a translation program of well-known classical reformers in Islam from the previous two centuries in an effort to instill in the rising generation the value of fusing good ideas from outside with Muslim cultures. Instead of hearing about Ibn Taymiyya from al-Qaʿida and radical clerics, the young generation would be reading about Jamal al-Din al-Afghani, Muhammad Abdu, and Rashid Rida as well as current thinkers. The translation project would also include works written in English in the United States and Britain about the compatibility of Islam and democracy and the new reasoning (*ijtihad*) that is being discussed among Muslim intellectuals in the West. Reformist publications and translations of foreign works should be sold at subsidized prices, and high school and college teachers should be strongly encouraged to include such writings in their curricula as required readings and to hold discussions on some of the ideas contained in them.

Expand American Cultural Centers

The proposal to open "America Houses" in other countries has merit and should be considered. Whether it is called "America House"—much like the British Council, Alliance Française, and

Russia House—or "The American Cultural Center," the United
States should seriously consider opening a number of these centers in Arab and Muslim countries, in both urban and rural areas. The cultural centers, which to some might appear as a rein-
carnation of the old U.S. Information Service, should be
established away from the U.S. Embassy, which in most countries has understandably become more of a "fortress America."
Unlike existing public affairs offices that in most countries operate out of the embassy, the proposed cultural centers should be
located near the city or town center and accessible to the average citizen; they should have an open-door policy without the
massive security presence that usually surrounds the embassy
grounds.

These centers would provide a library and a reading room,
Internet service, subsidized classes in English, computers, art,
and documentaries of life in America as a pluralistic, multiethnic, and multiracial country. The documentaries would also
chronicle the life of the Muslim community's multifaceted contributions to the economic, social, political, educational, scientific, and cultural life of the United States. The center would also
have a lecture hall for meetings, conferences, and debates on
topics that concern the local community and could invite local
groups to hold their meetings at the cultural centers. With such
facilities, these cultural centers could be transformed into "community centers" where the youth could go to read books, newspapers and magazines, attend a meeting, watch television, listen
to music, use the Internet, obtain information and forms about
educational exchange programs, play chess and other games,
and take classes at an affordable cost. These "community centers" should become the place where Americans and Muslims
can find common ground. Visitors would feel more comfortable
if the cultural centers are staffed by local employees, preferably
young, who in addition to their own language would to be fluent in English. These employees should act as informal emissar-
ies to the community, go out to local schools, and give talks on
topics of interest to local residents. On the Fourth of July and
other American and local festivals and holidays and feasts, the
cultural centers should open their doors to the community in

celebrations in which American diplomats from the embassy would participate. Public diplomacy through these activities would be the centerpiece of foreign policy involving every diplomat at the embassy. To succeed, public diplomacy must reflect a national commitment on the part of the U.S. government to reach out to the Muslim world. Success in cultural diplomacy would greatly assist in the fight against terrorism, and if staffed properly, the proposed American cultural centers could become a viable source of information about the United States and its values.

Partner Homeland Security with Local Communities

Although, at first glane, a recommendation on homeland security does not fall under public diplomacy, addressing domestic threats and the perception and treatment of American Muslims will have repercussions in Muslim countries. Terrorist threats to the homeland will not be adequately dealt with unless a functional partnership is established between federal government agencies and states and cities across the United States. In order for this partnership to be most effective, it must cover collection and analysis of data, sharing of information from all sources (to include satellite imagery and human intelligence), enhancement of expertise, and joint efforts to learn more about Islam and Muslims, as a religion and as citizens, and to fight off bigoted attitudes toward American Muslims. The proposed partnership should also include members of the Muslim community across American cities and towns. A recent Pew public opinion poll of American Muslims showed that many American Muslims are middle class and mostly mainstream. Although American Muslims are critical of American foreign policy, especially Iraq policy (which is not dissimilar to the views of a majority of Americans), they are widely concerned about Islamic extremism and terrorism and strongly oppose suicide bombings.

A summer 2007 report by the New York Police Department titled *Radicalization in the West: The Homegrown Threat* clearly shows that local communities, such as New York City, not only are concerned about the growth of extremism and the radical-

ization of Muslim youth but have developed sophisticated expertise in this area. Local communities must have the resources
and intelligence-based information to understand and track the
four stages of the radicalization process identified in the report
("pre-radicalization," "self-dentification," "indoctrination," and
"jihadization") and to focus on potential terrorists in their
midst. Once they have resources and intelligence, cities like
New York are less encumbered by federal bureaucracies and delays. The model outlined in this report can be applicable to other
major cities and must be studied thoroughly.

As the lines separating the international and domestic arenas
in the fight against terrorism become more blurred, commu-
nity-based intelligence, to use a phrase coined by a Los Alamos
scientist in a private conversation, assumes greater urgency.
Such an approach should be incorporated in the Intelligence
Reorganization Act and developed into a national policy. It
stands to reason that homeland security officials in New York
City, Chicago, Los Angeles, or Houston cannot discharge their
responsibilities adequately, especially in the area of Islamic activism, unless they are incorporated in the national decision-
making process, are provided the necessary information, and
are made to feel like true partners. Patronizing attitudes by federal bureaucrats toward local officials have not worked well in
the past and will spell disaster should another major terrorist
act occur. The recommendation to share nationally collected intelligence with domestic entities understandably might raise
concerns with civil liberties advocates, but the fact remains that
the traditional fire wall that separated the domestic responsibilities of the FBI and other law-enforcement agencies from those
of Central Intelligence (CIA, NSA, etc.) is no longer applicable.
The United States and the Islamic world are inextricably linked,
and anti-U.S. sentiments overseas are often carried to the United
States by disaffected Muslim youth and potential foreign terrorists. Religious ideologies among American Muslims tend to reflect the diversity, complexity, and sectarian tensions that characterize Islamic groups overseas, and the political, religious, and
social tensions that often exist in a particular congregation in
the United States usually mirror the tensions in other countries.

To address potential threats to the homeland at the state and local levels adequately, federal officials must share meaningful information about terror threats with their state and local counterparts and communicate with them regularly.

These recommendations will cost money and require a massive reshuffling of the organizational chart at the State Department, the NSC, and other agencies. Public diplomacy will not succeed if it is run on a shoestring budget with minimal reorganization. Unless U.S. policymakers view public diplomacy as central to U.S. national security, appropriate the necessary funds, and marshal public support for these national programs, the effort will not succeed and American credibility will remain suspect. Any policy revisions in the major foreign policy trouble spots must be aligned with new public diplomacy. A redesigned public diplomacy can help the country regain the stature, prestige, and influence it had in the Muslim world a few decades earlier and recapture its past image as a beacon for hope, liberty, and human dignity.

Conclusion

_____

LOOKING AHEAD

RESEARCH FOR THIS BOOK has shown that America's low standing in Muslim countries can be turned around. Public opinion data and numerous government and think tank reports in recent years also indicate that majorities of Muslims generally support good governance, seek to participate in the political process through open and free elections, and are committed to gradual, evolutionary change. They do not clash with the United States over ideas or values but over policies and would respond positively to a change in these policies. The public diplomacy blueprint offered in this book is a way forward, not a look backward. Polling data have shown that the policies of the past six years have put the United States on a collision course with the Islamic world and have undermined American credibility and stature worldwide. The United States should attempt to reverse this trend and reestablish American moral leadership and rekindle other nations' faith in this country's deep-rooted commitment to justice, fairness, the rule of law, civil rights, and international norms of behavior.

As my conversations with hundreds of Muslim interlocutors across the Islamic world have shown and public opinion polls have confirmed, winning wars and invading other countries, for whatever reason, do not make the world any safer and do not guarantee winning the hearts and minds of others. Having the world's most awesome military machine is not a substitute for diplomacy. In fact, the opposite has happened. Muslim and non-Muslim majorities of those interviewed in the polls viewed the United States as a threat to world peace and the world as less safe. The failure to establish a genuine democracy in Iraq and make it an exemplar of tolerance and pluralism for the region, coupled with pulling U.S. troops out of Iraq without achieving the lofty goals enunciated by the administration more than five

years ago, could prompt the United States to move toward res-
urrecting a functional system of multilateral diplomacy. Such
an initiative would be a pleasure for public diplomacy officials
to sell. While the military has been the key element of American
power in the past six years, the United States should now work
toward building a new international consensus for regional and
global stability that will be anchored in diplomacy and other
elements of power, including public diplomacy. A U.S.-led rein-
vigorated international partnership is the only sure defense
against terrorism and other acts of global lawlessness.

The Baker-Hamilton Iraq Study Group report captured the
need for diplomacy best when it called on the United States to
"embark on a robust diplomatic effort to establish an international support structure intended to stabilize Iraq and ease tensions in other countries in the region." This critical recommendation could apply to American relations with other parts of the
world and should inform the United States diplomatic agenda.
Although the 9/11 terrorist attacks against the United States
and other terrorist acts since September 2001 against Indonesia,
Egypt, Jordan, Morocco, Saudi Arabia, Kenya, Tanzania, Britain, and Spain have soured relations between the Islamic world
and the West because of the involvement of Islamic radicals in
these attacks, recent developments in the Islamic world offer
hopeful signs for the future, and the United States should be
positioned to capitalize on these signs and incorporate them in
a new public diplomacy.

Some of the hopeful signs include the expanding debate
within the Islamic world regarding the role of violence in Islam,
the need to open up the doors of *ijtihad*, the growing rejection
of the radical paradigm—including suicide bombings, the killing of innocent civilians, all forms of terrorism, and above all
al-Qa'ida's views of the Islamic political community—by majorities of Muslims, increasing demands for political reform and
democratization, a growing interest among Islamic political
parties to participate in the political process regardless of the
nature of the regime, and a growing debate among Muslim communities in non-Muslim countries to reconcile their faith and
their active citizenship in those countries. This assessment is

not Pollyannaish; it recognizes the continued influence of al-Qa'ida and the radical clerics, or the enablers of jihadist terrorism, among the youth and the allure of the promises they make in recruiting young men to commit murder in the name of religion. However, the radicalization and intolerance of the few should not obscure the tolerance and pragmatism of the many.

The June 2007 election of the AKP in Turkey is a good example of a political party that simultaneously can be true to its Islamic roots and defend the secular nature of the Turkish state. Although the Muslim Brotherhood has vastly different historical, cultural, and local experiences than the AKP, the ongoing discussions within the Brotherhood regarding the establishment of its own political party should include study of the AKP experience and the relationship between it and the state. One is encouraged by the centrist ideologies of Islamic political parties across the Islamic world and their growing interest in becoming active players in their political systems.

As Muslims live all over the world and as the classical world of Islam is becoming much more diffused geographically and culturally, Islamic thought is being influenced by ideas from the Americas, Western Europe, Australia, India, China, Japan, and other places. The intermeshing of ideas at the popular level and the inadvertent cross-fertilization of conversations and thought processes will in the long term help dilute exclusivist extremism and move people's thought—religious and nonreligious—to the center. Today, vast majorities of Muslims live outside the Arab heartland of Islam in non-Muslim or nominally Muslim states, and the abode of Islam or *dar al-Islam* is no longer a defined geographic entity but largely a state of mind. Whereas in the late nineteenth and early twentieth centuries only a few Muslim intellectuals and reformist thinkers—for example, Jamal al-Din al-Afghani, Muhammad Abdu, Rashid Rida, and Taha Hussein—were exposed to, and benefited from, ideas that came from outside the domain of Islam, today millions of Muslims are exposed to these ideas and on a daily basis incorporate them in their personal lives. Herein lies the hope for Islamic modernism and for the ultimate marginalization of radical thought. Another encouraging sign of the debate is the growing ideological disagreement between Islamic activists in specific countries and the global radical teachings of al-Qa'ida. Most Islamic political parties and activists have focused on national agendas within their own states and have to accept the validity of nation-states, albeit Islamic in orientation, whereas al-Qa'ida and radical clerics have been committed to a universal Islamic caliphate. The two sides are diametrically opposed in their view of the polity and the role of Islam in it, with al-Qa'ida on the losing side and "nationalist" Islamic parties on the winning side. The more Islamic parties enter the political fray, the more unappealing al-Qa'ida's ideology becomes. These positive developments lead me to believe that this book might be equally useful to educated audiences in the Muslim world as well. College and university students and teachers, civil society and political party activists, and other professionals could use the book to search for common ground on their side of the policy and civilizational chasm because, for American-Muslim engagement to work and endure, the two sides will have to work through their common concerns about current policy, the challenges of terrorism they both face, and the aspirations for prosperity, the good life, and human dignity.

The public diplomacy recommendations are based on the assumption that American policymakers must develop extensive expertise and experience in Muslim societies and cultures and have clear goals and realistic expectations before they embark on a comprehensive public policy program. The recommendations will require acceptance by the U.S. Congress and the American people and should engage the American Muslim community; that is to say, the president will need to explain the reasons behind this envisioned public diplomacy and how such an initiative would serve the national interest and security of the United States. The presidential message should, of course, be conveyed to the Muslim world through the newly appointed ambassador to the Organization of the Islamic Conference. Some of the recommendations will be controversial requiring new initiatives; others would build on what is already being done on a smaller scale. But all of them will require many millions of dollars to implement. It is tempting to say that most of the recommendations could be financed by what the United States government spent in Iraq in one month in 2007. More fundamental than the moneys required is the conviction that reaching out to the Muslim world is good for America and for Muslims and will help in the hunt for terrorist criminals. Through a daring, creative, and comprehensive public diplomacy, the United States can stand tall and justly reclaim its moral standing in the world.

ACKNOWLEDGMENTS

AFTER RETIRING from the Central Intelligence Agency and after talking to a number of colleagues and friends in government and in academia, the idea of a book about how we as a government can better communicate with the Muslim world began to crystallize in my mind. The hundreds of anecdotes I collected from my conversations with Muslim interlocutors over the years and the polling data collected from the Pew, the Gallup, and other public opinion polls convinced me that I have a story to tell and that I could offer useful recommendations on strategic relations between the United States and Muslim peoples and societies. Many people, directly and indirectly, contributed to the writing of the book, but most unfortunately will remain anonymous because of their employment, social and political positions, the countries they live in, the electronic and print media they work for, and the groups they are affiliated with. I owe a debt of gratitude to many Muslim interlocutors (professionals, academics, thinkers, clerics, religious leaders, civil society and political party activists, booksellers, and average people) across dozens of countries for their time and willingness to share their thoughts, hopes, frustrations, and aspirations with me. I learned much from their analysis of where the Islamic world is heading and of what future Muslims envision for their faith. My thanks also go to diplomats, former colleagues, and friends at numerous American embassies for facilitating my travels and meetings and for informing me about the countries I visited and the individuals I met. I am especially grateful to my former colleagues who are still gainfully employed in the intelligence and policy communities in Washington and elsewhere for their friendship and support. I am proud to have known them and worked with them. I would like to recognize a few special former colleagues for their encouragement, ideas, support, and friendship before and since retirement from government service: Dave Carey, Hank Crumpton, Jami Miscik, John Moseman, George Tenet, Winston Wiley, and Tom Wolfe.

My thanks also go to many academic colleagues for sharing their ideas and analytic insights into Muslim societies, cultures, and ideologies over the years and for informing my analysis of Islamic political activism and of specific Muslim countries. I would like to recognize a few of them for the warm friendship I have established with them over the years, the privilege of knowing them, and the special support they provided in making the U.S. government's academic outreach such a success: Bahman Baktiari, Ali Banuazizi, Dale Eickelman, John Esposito, Bob Hefner, Farhad Kazemi, Vali Nasr, Richard Norton, Mark Tessler, and John Voll.

Special thanks go to the Princeton University Press team, especially to Fred Appel who encouraged me to write the book and helped me greatly in preparing the proposal in a "nonbureaucratic" language. I am also grateful to the members of the editorial staff for their personal interest in the manuscript, precision, and punctuality.

Finally, my family deserves a special word of thanks. My wife, Ilonka, supported the book project from its inception, although she anticipated that the writing would reduce our hiking time in the Sandias; she also read several drafts and offered insightful suggestions. Our daily conversations about "why I was writing the book and for whom" helped me tremendously in sharpening the main message of the book. On a recent road trip to the Grand Canyon, my two sons, Charlie and Richard, contributed to the book conversation by asking probing questions and making thoughtful suggestions, especially relating to the blueprint recommendations.

GLOSSARY

'Adl — (justice); *'adalat* or *'adil* in Muslim countries outside the Arab world. It is a very important concept in Islam, and several Islamic political parties and movements use this word in their official name.

Ahl al-Bayt — (people of the house of the Prophet Muhammad). The group from which the successor to Muhammad should hail, according to Shia Islam. It is also an Iranian-supported organization that promotes Shia proselytization and pro-Iranian activities in Muslim countries, especially in sub-Saharan Africa and Central Asia.

'Ashura — The tenth of the Muslim month of Muharram when Shia Muslims commemorate the martyrdom of Imam Husayn, son of the fourth Caliph 'Ali and grandson of the Prophet Muhammad, at Karbala (modern-day Iraq) in 680 C.E.

Ayatollah — (Sign of God). The title of a highly respected Shia religious scholar.

bay'a — The Muslim community's declaration of allegiance to the incoming leader of the community or the ruler.

dar al-harb — (house of war). A reference to non-Muslim territory.

dar al-Islam — (house of Islam). A reference to Muslim territory.

da'wa — (call Islamic). Proselytization of the faith; written *dakwa* in Southeast Asia.

Deoband — A Muslim school of thought and a body of belief in South Asia. The major Deoband university is located outside Delhi, India.

fiqh — Islamic jurisprudence.

fatwa — Formal legal opinion or ruling on a religious question, ranging from personal hygiene to violent jihad, by a *mufti* or a religious leader authorized to issue a *fatwa*. In recent years, *fatwas* have been issued by radical leaders, such as Usama Bin Ladin, who are not qualified to issue *fatwas*.

fitna — (burn). In political situations, the term refers to sedition, social unrest, or antiregime activities.

Fuqaha' al-jihad — (scholars of jihad). Saudi and other radical clerics who have issued *fatwas* or other rulings justifying violent jihad against "enemies" of Islam.

Hadith — Narrative report or sayings of the Prophet Muhammad; *Sahih al-Bukhari*, written in the ninth century C.E., is a major source of Hadith.

halal — Lawful or permitted activities or actions in Islam. It also refers to foods prepared according to Islamic laws and practices.

haram — Unlawful or prohibited activities or activities in Islam.

al-Haramayn — A formerly Saudi-financed nongovernmental organization, which in recent years has been associated with radical activities. The name is a reference to Islam's two most sacred shrines in Mecca and Medina in Saudi Arabia.

hawza — A place or a learning center where senior Shia scholars or ayatollahs gather to study and teach. Shia *hawzas* today exist in Najaf and Karbala in Iraq and in Qom in Iran.

hiraba — (war against society). A term used by antiterrorist religious scholars to refer to the criminal acts of terrorists. After 9/11 several prominent Islamic scholars denounced the terrorist acts and called them *hiraba,* implying that terrorism was a violation of Islamic norms and should be considered a crime against humanity.

Hizb al-Tahrir — (Islamic liberation party). Active in Southeast Asia, Central Asia, the Middle East, Western Europe, and other places, the party advocates a restoration of the caliphate.

'Id al-'Adha — (festival of sacrifice). The last day of the *hajj* and the most significant religious feast in Sunni Islam.

'Id al-Fitr — (festival of the breaking of the fast). Falls at the end of the holy month of Ramadan in the Islamic calendar.

ijtihad — (reasoning or independent analysis of sources of the faith). Traditional Sunni Islam believes that the door of *ijtihad* had closed after the development of the four schools of jurisprudence in the ninth century C.E. Some contemporary Sunni Muslim scholars, outside the Arab Islamic heartland, are engaged in *ijtihad* as part of the ongoing debate within Islam. In Shia Islam, *ijtihad* is a religious interpretation or reasoning done by a qualified, well-established scholar or ayatollah. The person engaged in *ijtihad* is called a *mujtahid,* a highly respected title for Shia Muslims.

imam — a religiously trained person who leads people in prayer. In Shia Islam, *imam* refers to the successor of Muhammad, which applies to 'Ali and his descendants.

islah — (reform or revitalization). The term is often used in the names of Islamic political parties as in the Islah Party in Yemen.

Islamization—Muslims' awareness of their Islamic identity. Also refers to social and political actions justified by specific interpretations of Islam.

jahiliyya — (ignorance). A period of ignorance of the One God in pre-Islamic Arabia. It is used by some contemporary radical thinkers, most notably Sayyid Qutb, to refer to the "un-Islamic" behavior of Muslim rulers.

jihad — (holy struggle). Applies to a religious or physical activity from strengthening the faith of individual Muslims, for example, deepening one's faith through increased piety, to defending Islam by all means, including the use of violence. The term also refers to armed struggle or holy war; "jihadists," or "mujahidin" are those engaged in lawful or unlawful violent jihad.

kafir — (unbeliever); plural *kuffar*.

Khalifa — Caliph or successor to the Prophet Muhammad. The first four "rightly guided" Caliphs after Muhammad—Abu Bakr, 'Umar, 'Uthman, and 'Ali—are considered by Sunni Islam the true "salaf" or ancestors of Islam. 'Ali is most revered by Shia Islam and is referred to as the first *Imam*.

Khilafa — The system of Islamic government that is headed by a caliph.

madrasa — An Islamic religious or Qur'anic school.

marja'-e taqlid — (source of imitation or emulation). A leading scholar or *mujtahid* in Shia Islam whose interpretation should be followed.

masjid — Mosque or a place of worship for Muslims.

al-Masjid al-'Aqsa—(farthest mosque). The name the Qur'an gives to the Temple Mount in Jerusalem. Muslims believe that the Prophet Muhammad took a one-night journey to heaven from the Sacred mosque in Mecca through the Temple of Solomon in Jerusalem (Qur'an, 17:1); it was the place of worship farthest west known to the Arabs at the time of the Prophet.

Ramadan — The most sacred month in the Islamic calendar during which Muslims fast from sunrise to sunset.

Salafi — Refers to Muslims who turn to the "pious ancestors" (*salaf* in Arabic) or the first four "rightly guided" Caliphs as the source of their faith. The movement is called Salafiyya.

shahada — Profession of faith and one of the five pillars of Islam. The other four are prayer, fasting, almsgiving, and pilgrimage to Mecca or *hajj*; radical thinkers claim that *jihad* is the sixth pillar.

Sharia — Islamic law and jurisprudence.

Schools of Jurisprudence — Four major schools of jurisprudence in Sunni Islam named after their founders that offer different interpretations of Islamic law and procedure (Hanafi after Abu-Hanifa, 699–767 C.E.; Maliki after Malik bin Anas, 714–98 C.E.; Shafi'i after al-Shafi'i, 767–820 C.E.; and Hanbali after Ahmad ibn Hanbal, 780–855 C.E.). The Hanafi school tends to be the most liberal, and the Hanbali the most conservative.

tajdid — Renewal or revival of Islam through *ijtihad* or independent analysis of theological sources; also refers to reformist thought in contemporary Islam.

takfir — Declaring a person or a group unbelievers, thereby justifying killing them. Radical Sunnis have used this tool against their opponents.

tawhid — Oneness of God and the universe and His absolute sovereignty over all creation. It is the basic religious doctrine of Wahhabism and also one of the tenets of the radical Sunni paradigm.

ulama — Muslim religious scholars; plural of *alim*.

umma — Muslim community; refers to worldwide Islamic community. The term is used often by radical thinkers to refer to global jihad.

Velayat-e Faqih — Guardianship or government by an expert in Shia Islam. The title was introduced by Ayatollah Khomeini in Iran after the removal of the Shah in 1979.

Wahhabi — Refers to a follower of Muhammad ibn Abd al-Wahhab, a Saudi conservative thinker in the eighteenth century. The movement is called Wahhabiyya or Wahhabism.

Wahhabism — A theological interpretation of Islam founded by Muhammad ibn Abd al-Wahhab in Arabia in the eighteenth century—offers a narrow, conservative, strict, and literal interpretation of Islam revolving around the concept of *tawhid* (oneness of God), which teaches that God alone is the creator, provider, and disposer of the universe. Wahhabism, a term used interchangeably with Salafism in Saudi Arabia, is intolerant of the other monotheistic religions, believes that Islam is the only way to salvation, and urges Muslims to view Jews and Christians as potential enemies and not to interact with them. It calls on its followers to make a commitment (*iltizam*) to Islam, undergo training to strengthen their religious commitment, and participate in jihad on behalf of Islam. Having been in control of the public and religious school curricula in Saudi Arabia, the Salafis have established a Wahhabi or Salafi-based curriculum and nurtured generations of Saudi youth grounded in this type of education.

wasatiyya — (at the center) or *wasat*. A centrist or mainstream political ideology advocated by several Islamic political parties.

SOURCES CITED

Ali Engineer, Asghar. 2005. *Theory and Practice of the Islamic State*. Lahore, Pakistan: Vanguard Books.

Al-Anani, Khalil. 2007. "Is 'Brotherhood' with America Possible?" *Arab Insight* 1 (1): 7–17.

Ansari, Ali. 2006. *Confronting Iran: The Failure of American Foreign Policy and the Next Great Conflict in the Middle East*. New York: Basic Books.

Aslan, Reza. 2006. *No god but God: The Origins, Evolution, and Future of Islam*. New York: Random House.

Baker, James, III, and Lee Hamilton. 2006. *The Iraq Study Group Report: The Way Forward—A New Approach*. New York: Vintage Books.

BBC News. http://news.bbc.co.uk. Published February 19, 2007.

Cole, Juan. 2007. *Napoleon's Egypt: Invading the Middle East*. New York: Palgrave Macmillan.

Cultural Diplomacy: The Linchpin of Public Diplomacy; Report of the Advisory Committee on Cultural Diplomacy. 2005. Washington, D.C., U.S. Department of State.

Delong-Bas, Natana. 2004. *Wahhabi Islam: From Revival and Reform to Global Jihad*. New York: Oxford University Press.

Djerijian, Edward. 1992. "The US and the Middle East in a Changing World." Address at Meridian House International, June 2, 1992. *Dispatch*, (23) (June 8, 1992).

———. 2003. *Advisory Commission on Public Diplomacy*. Washington, D.C.: Department of State. www.state.gov.

Doumato, Eleanor, and Gregory Starett, eds. 2007. *Teaching Islam: Textbooks and Religion in the Middle East*. New York: Lynne Reinner Publishers.

Eickelman, Dale, and Piscatori, James. 2004. *Muslim Politics*. 2nd ed. Princeton, N.J.: Princeton University Press.

Esposito, John. 1998. *Islam: The Straight Path*. New York: Oxford University Press.

———. 2002. *Unholy War: Terror in the Name of Islam*. New York: Oxford University Press.

Al-Fahd, Nasir Bin Hamid. May 2003. *A Treatise on the Legal Status of Using Weapons of Mass Destruction against Infidels* [Arabic]. Riyadh, Saudi Arabia.

"15-Nation Pew Global Attitudes Survey." 2006. The Pew Global Attitudes Survey. www.pewglobal.org.

"Gallup World Poll: Islam and Democracy, Selected Findings from 10 Predominantly Muslim Countries." 2006. Princeton, N.J.: Gallup Organization.

Gerges, Fawaz. 2006. *Journey of the Jihadist.* New York: Harcourt.

Hefner, Robert. 2000. *Civil Islam: Muslims and Democratization in Indonesia.* Princeton, N.J.: Princeton University Press.

Hersh, Seymour. 2004. *Chain of Command: The Road from 9/11 to Abu Ghraib.* New York: HarpersCollins.

"How Do We Collect Intelligence?" 2007. Washington, D.C.: Office of the Director of National Intelligence. http://www.dni.gov.

Johnston, Rob. 2005. *Analytic Culture in the U.S. Intelligence Community.* Washington, D.C.: CIA, Center for the Study of Intelligence.

Klein, Menachem. 2007. "Hamas in Power." *Middle East Journal* 61 (3): 442–59.

Kohut, Andrew, and Bruce Stokes. 2006. *America against the World: How We Are Different and Why We Are Disliked.* New York: Times Books.

Lilla. Mark. 2007. "The Politics of God." *New York Times Magazine,* August 19, 28–35, 50–55.

Lustick, Ian. 2006. *Trapped in the War on Terror.* Philadelphia: University of Pennsylvania Press.

"Muslim Americans: Middle Class and Mostly Mainstream." 2007. Washington, D.C.: Pew Research Center. www.pewresearchcenter.org.

"Muslim Public Opinion on US Policy, Attacks on Civilians and the Al Qaeda." 2007. College Park, Md.: World Public Opinion.org, Program on International Policy Studies, University of Maryland.

Nasr, Vali. 2006. *The Shia Revival: How Conflicts within Islam Will Shape the Future.* New York: W. W. Norton.

———. 1996. *Mawdudi and the Making of Islamic Revivalism.* New York: Oxford University Press.

"National Intelligence Estimate: The Terrorist Threat to the US Homeland." July 2007. Declassified Key Judgments. Washington, D.C.: National Intelligence Council. http://www.dni.gov.

New Frontiers of Intelligence Analysis: Shared Threats, Diverse Perspectives, New Communities. 2004. Washington, D.C.: CIA, Sherman Kent School for Intelligence Analysis.

Norton, Augustus Richard. 2007. *Hizbollah: A Short History.* Princeton, N.J.: Princeton University Press.

Oren, Michael. 2007. *Power, Faith, and Fantasy: America in the Middle East, 1776 to the Present.* New York: W. W. Norton.

Perle, Richard. 2007. "How the CIA Failed America." *Washington Post,* May 11, A19.

Power, Samantha. 2007. "Our War on Terror." *New York Times Book Review,* July, 29, 1, 8.

Radicalization in the West: The Homegrown Threat. 2007. New York: NYPD, Intelligence Division, City of New York, Police Department.

Report to the President of the United States. 2005. Washington, D.C.: Commission on the Intelligence Capabilities of the United States Regarding Weapons of Mass Destruction.

A Review of U.S. Counterterrorism Policy: American Muslim Critique and Recommendations. 2003. Washington, D.C.: Muslim Public Affairs Council.

Sen, Amartya. 2006. *Identity and Violence: The Illusion of Destiny.* New York: W. W. Norton.

Shahrur, Muhammad. 1994. *Contemporary Islamic Studies in State and Society* [Arabic.] Damascus, Syria: al-Ahali.

Silverstein, Ken. 2007. "Parties of God: The Bush Doctrine and the Rise of Islamic Democracy." *Harper's Magazine,* March, 33–44.

Simon, Steven. 2007. *After the Surge: The Case for US Military Disengagement from Iraq.* New York: Council on Foreign Relations.

Sims, Jennifer E., and Burton Gerber, eds. 2006. *Transforming U.S. Intelligence.* Washington, D.C.: Georgetown University Press.

"Strengthening Our Friendship with the Muslim Community Worldwide": President Bush Rededicates the Islamic Center of Washington. June 27, 2007. Washington, D.C.: The White House.

Takeyh, Ray. 2006. *Hidden Iran: Paradox and Power in the Islamic Republic.* New York: Times Books.

Tenet, George. 2007. *At the Center of the Storm: My Years at the CIA.* New York: HarperCollins.

Traub, James. 2007. "Islamic Democrats?" *New York Times Magazine,* April 29, 44–49.

Wallach, Janet. 2005. *Desert Queen: The Extraordinary Life of Gertrude Bell, Adventurer, Adviser to Kings, Ally of Lawrence of Arabia.* London: Orion Publishing.

"The War We Need to Win." Remarks of Senator Obama at the Wilson Center. August 1, 2007. Washington, D.C.: BarakObama.com. www.barakobama.com/2007/08/01.

Warde, Ibrahim. 2007. *The Price of Fear: Al-Qaeda and the Truth behind the Financial War on Terror.* New York: I. B. Tauris.

Wiktorowicz, Quintan. 2005. "A Genealogy of Radical Islam." *Studies in Conflict & Terrorism* 28: 75–97.

Yilmaz, Hakan. 2007. "Islam, Sovereignty, and Democracy: A Turkish View." *Middle East Journal* 61 (3): 477–93.

INDEX

Abbas, Mahmoud, 95–96
Abdu, Muhammad, 17, 111, 135, 142
Abu Ghraib, xviii, 98, 105
al-Afghani, Jamal al-Din, 17, 111, 135, 142
Afghanistan: jihadists produced in, 43; Muslim perceptions of U.S. invasion of, 84; resurgence of the Taliban and al-Qaʿida in, 81, 87
AKP. *See* Justice and Development Party (Turkey)
al-Alaʾ Mawdudi, Abu, 13
Algeria, 42
al-Ali, Hamid, 13, 117
al-Qaʿida: democracy, repudiation of, 91; global jihad advocated by, 6; growing threat from, 80–82; Hamas, criticism of, 63; Muslim perceptions of goals of, 76–77; Muslim public opinion vs. views of, 73; "nationalist" Islamic parties vs., 143; participation of Islamic parties in elections, opposition to, 94; post-invasion Iraq and, 58, 86; radical Islamic activism voiced by spokesmen of, 12–14; the sixth stage of Islamization and, 12; violence, permissibility of, 13–14; weapons of mass destruction, argument for acquisition of, 14–16
al-Qaʿida in Iraq, 86
American Association of Higher Education, 133–34
American cultural centers in Muslim countries, 135–37
American University of Beirut, 132–33
Amin, Qasim, 111
Arabism, Islam and, 18–21, 49
Arkun, Muhammad, 17, 111

Ataturk, Mustapha Kemal, 5, 116
al-Awda, Salman, 13, 29, 115
Azzam, Abdallah, 13

Bahrain, 26–27. *See also* Wifaq Party
Baker-Hamilton Iraq Study Group (ISG), 95–96, 141
al-Barrak, Abd al-Rahman bin Nasir, 13, 29, 117
Bin Ladin, Usama: American soldiers in Saudi Arabia, opposition to, 43; attitudes of Muslim majority vs. views of, 73; global jihad against the U.S. advocated by, 6, 13–14, 19; Husayn and, no evidence of ties between, 58; killing of innocent civilians, argument justifying, 115; Muslim Caliphate, call for restoration of, 116; Muslim youth, appeal to, 16; radical paradigm, articulator of, 12–13; symbolism of continued life and communications of, 81–82
Blair, Tony, 41
Brown, Gordon, xviii
Bush, George W.: "Crusade," use of the word, 103; envoy to the OIC, appointment of, xii–xiii; international perceptions of, 78–79; link between Iraq and al-Qaʿida, claims regarding, 58; outreach to Muslims, 101, 120; pro-democracy speeches by, 90
Bush administration: CIA intelligence, reactions to, 54; Iraq, failure to acknowledge insurgency in, 57–58; Iraq invasion, commitment to, 54–56, 59–60; Muslim perceptions of, 74, 88; Palestine, disappearance of "honest broker" role in, 97; unilateralism of, 98

Wahhabi Islam: beliefs of, 116; Salafis'
adherence to, 113; Saudi Arabia and,
20–21; spread of, 8
war on terrorism. *See* global war on
terror
weapons of mass destruction (WMD):
Islamic radicals' justification for acquiring and using, 14–16; Muslim
opinions regarding, 78
Wifaq Party (Bahrain), 26, 31, 92
WMD. *See* weapons of mass destruction
WMD Commission. *See* Commission

of the Intelligence Capabilities of the
United States Regarding Weapons of
Mass Destruction
World Assembly of Muslim Youth, 21

Zakzaki, 22
al-Zawahiri, Ayman: global jihad advocated by, 6; participation of Islamic parties in elections, opposition to, 94; radical Islamic message
voiced by, 13; symbolism of continued life and communications of,
81–82